The Growth Leader

Strategies to Drive
the Top and Bottom Lines

The
Growth
Leader

Scott K. Edinger

**FAST
COMPANY**
Press

Fast Company Press
New York, New York
www.fastcompanypress.com

This work is being published under the Fast Company Press imprint by an exclusive arrangement with Fast Company. Fast Company and the Fast Company logo are registered trademarks of Mansueto Ventures, LLC. The Fast Company Press logo is a wholly owned trademark of Mansueto Ventures, LLC.

Distributed by Greenleaf Book Group

For ordering information or special discounts for bulk purchases, please contact Greenleaf Book Group at PO Box 91869, Austin, TX 78709, 512.891.6100.

Design and composition by Greenleaf Book Group
Cover design by Greenleaf Book Group

Publisher's Cataloging-in-Publication data is available.

Print ISBN: 978-1-63908-047-2

eBook ISBN: 978-1-63908-048-9

To offset the number of trees consumed in the printing of our books, Greenleaf donates a portion of the proceeds from each printing to the Arbor Day Foundation. Greenleaf Book Group has replaced over 50,000 trees since 2007.

Printed in the United States of America on acid-free paper

23 24 25 26 27 28   10 9 8 7 6 5 4 3 2 1

First Edition

To my wife, Christy, and our children,
Ava and Vivienne, with love

Contents

Foreword

A great organizational scholar, James March, emphasized that "leadership involves plumbing as well as poetry." His point was that, whatever else they do, effective leaders help people in their firms to deal behaviorally with opportunities and problems and thus increase their contributions and productivity. This is especially true when it comes to the lifeblood of a company: the acquisition and retention of customers. Yet, many leaders are out of touch with their firms' sales activities and practices. C-suites are increasingly siloed among specialists, and more senior executives than ever have made it to the top without prolonged customer-contact experience throughout their careers.

This gap affects a core leadership task: formulating and implementing a market-relevant strategy. To stay in business, any business must be about customer value and tailoring its activities to serve target customers better or differently than others. But surveys indicate that less than 50 percent of employees say they understand their firm's strategy, and the percentage *decreases* the closer you get to the customer in responses from sales and service employees. Sales is often treated as a mysterious black box—essential, but a tactical tool that's rarely part of strategy formulation. Moreover, many sales leaders like it that way. It's a dialogue that never happens, and *that's* how companies get disrupted.

To close this gap, you must treat causes, not symptoms, and Scott Edinger's *The Growth Leader* can help you to do that. As Edinger notes, "Sales is strategy in action." Profitable growth is ultimately an organizational outcome, requiring leaders to clarify and communicate priorities. Conversely, there is no such thing as effective selling if it's not connected to strategic goals. It's a two-way street.

Strategic priorities are about the choices a company makes as it competes in a market. Some choices are explicit in a plan, but many are implicit in daily decisions about resource allocations. For example, any budget involves choices about what gets more or less of available resources, and any sales model makes choices: money and time spent pursuing account A are not available for accounts B, C, and so on. The inevitability and impact of opportunity costs are most real in sales, and you must set and communicate priorities to the salesforce. A vague or unarticulated set of choices cannot be tested as markets change. People talk in abstractions ("innovate!"), while daily call patterns enact the sunk cost fallacy: throwing good money after bad. If priorities are implicit in the intuition of even a charismatic leader, then strategy execution is only as strong as that leader's reach and, more often, as weak as the weakest link in the organization. Over time, the firm becomes a global mediocrity: good at many things, but not especially good at any particular things. And the essence of competitive advantage is being very good at things your customers value and that others find hard to imitate.

Then, the issue is aligning behaviors with goals. Alignment is a set of processes, not a teamwork speech. It requires ongoing customer information for strategy development and, in execution, relevant performance management processes. Senior leaders establish the foundational conditions for alignment, and Edinger can help you complement vision and purpose with good organizational plumbing in areas like customer selection, value delivery, coaching, milestones for tracking progress (or not), and other aspects of execution. His Five Flag Start framework should be part of your strategy meetings because it provides a process for translating ideas into actions and decisions.

Finally, *The Growth Leader* is a book for managers, not pundits or "strategy priests" with abstract theories about competition. Edinger provides diagnostics that the C-suite can use to monitor and be involved in a productive way with customers and prospects. My experience on boards is that quarterly financial results are tracked closely. But the information needed to improve a key driver of bottom-line outcomes—how the sales force frames and delivers the value proposition—is often lacking. Or even worse, sales metrics emphasize volume, while senior executives believe their strategy is about premium value. If a leadership team can't make these connections between strategy and sales, it can end up pressing for better execution when the firm really needs a more market-relevant strategy or changing strategic direction when it should be focusing on selling basics.

Executives can't afford to leave this process to chance. Their oversight is as important here as it is in the capital budgeting process. Leadership groups who do not stay engaged with these processes will inevitably share the fate of companies where customer focus is a perennial slogan but not reality. It indeed starts at the top. *The Growth Leader* can spur necessary dialogue and help align a company's sales efforts and investments with its business goals.

—Frank V. Cespedes teaches at Harvard Business School and is the author
of *Aligning Strategy and Sales* and *Sales Management That Works*.

Don't Delegate This Book

This is a leadership book about business growth. It is not a sales book. The mere mention of sales in a business book often changes the category from leadership to sales, but I assure you that this book is for you. Yes, you'll see the word "sales" frequently enough in these pages, especially with regard to your relationship to the sales organization. But if your business relies on a professional sales team to connect with your customers, growth and sales are inextricably linked. If you hand this book off to your sales team or to your sales leadership without reading it yourself, you're making a huge mistake. Based on research you'll see soon, it is a mistake that may cause you to miss out on winning 25 to 53 percent more of the buying decision criteria and on active, engaged, and loyal customers. If you delegate this book down the line, you've already missed the point: Only *you*, as a senior leader, have the power to direct your company to continuous and sustainable success.

Sales leaders, give this book back to your CEO

If you are a VP or manager of sales and your CEO just asked you to review this book, please turn around, go back into their office, and show them this note. I'd suggest you share this copy or consider getting another and both read it so you can discuss the concepts like a small book club. You will probably agree with many of the sentiments expressed here, but only your company's most senior executives and decision-makers can drive these kinds of organization-wide changes. The book will be even more useful once your CEO has internalized its message. You won't be able to do it without their full support. Tell them I sent you.

Keep in mind that we're using sales as a featured example here. Many of the frameworks in this book apply to your entire organization, but the sales function holds the particular distinction of being frequently misunderstood by executives who view it only as a function of distribution rather than as a powerful differentiator. If you share that attitude, it is holding you back from connecting with your company's lifeline—the customer and prospects who are not yet customers. Sales is just another part of the whole. To focus your whole company on growth, you must bring all of its pieces together. That crucially includes leadership and sales.

Growth is a leadership issue, not a sales issue. Although many CEOs are focused on the bottom line, they often overlook the fact that the best way to drive bottom-line performance is to start with a healthy top line. Sustained, strategic growth—whether that means total revenue volume, net income growth, margin expansion, increased numbers of products or services, improved Net Promoter Scores, or other measures of customer loyalty[1]—requires an organization to do more than sell by communicating the value of products or services. It must create value in the way it sells. An organization must help customers with insights, expertise, and experience that provide real solutions to help customers achieve their objectives. It must deliver a compelling experience that adds value beyond the product itself. And as CEO, it's your job to guide that experience. Since growth is central to the execution of your strategy, few sales organizations could create an excellent sales experience without your leadership.

A recent study shows that 28 percent of CEOs adopt a hands-off policy with sales, another 40 percent are involved in an ad hoc way, and 18 percent focus on dealmaking while doing little else to coordinate with sales or support customer relationships.[2] Only 14 percent are strategically involved as Growth Leaders, collaborating with and supporting their sales organization. Put another way, a full 86 percent of CEOs do nothing to align sales with strategy. Sales is the execution of your strategy in the field—every day, hundreds or thousands of times each day—and that 86 percent disconnect is a problem. The C-suite—including you—must be appropriately involved with every department and must provide strategic leadership to each functional leadership team to ensure the successful execution of the company's go-to-market strategy.

A Growth Leader, however, knows that profitable growth lies at the intersection of strategy, leadership, and sales. Without a clear strategy, inspiring leadership, and aligned sales, you're likely to join that 86 percent of disconnected CEOs.

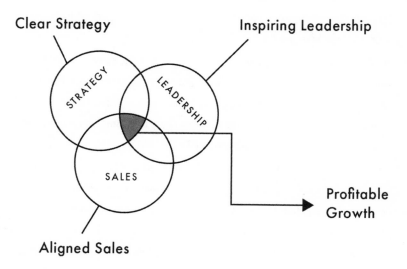

I rarely encounter pushback on the broad idea that growth—particularly, profitable revenue growth and margin expansion—is the responsibility of leadership. But beyond the lip service given to the idea, many executives are quick to delegate and even abdicate those results to the sales organization. The pushback I do get is about getting involved; the C-suite doesn't usually want to participate much with sales. The top leadership in most companies does not adequately understand what is required for a sales team to succeed today. They often believe that the primary—possibly the sole—purpose of the sales force is to generate revenue. They're wrong—or, at least, that mindset is woefully inadequate to compete in today's market. Some CEOs even protest, impatiently albeit honestly, that sellers "just need to get out there and sell." Sometimes I respond with a question—an often annoying question borrowed from Dr. Phil: "How is that working for you?"

Of course, the successful result of a great sales team is revenue—profitable revenue at that. While that is absolutely among the most important results produced by the sales team, it is not its purpose. That is akin to saying that the purpose of the finance team is to improve cash flow or reduce costs. Sure, those tasks are important responsibilities of the finance team, but it's a narrow view of their role in a business. It doesn't convey the fullness and depth of their greatest contribution to results. The purpose of a sales organization is to create value for customers and to connect a company's products and services to the business outcomes customers want to achieve, which is what turns them into a solution for the customer. This is a necessary part of designing and delivering a valuable and compelling sales experience. That sales experience sets your business apart from the competition, both in what you offer and how you offer it. Done well, that sales experience will influence buyer behavior and ultimately create more than your fair share of revenue—profitable revenue with the right kinds of customers.

Frustration with your sales organization is understandable, especially if you are disappointed with the numbers those sellers are turning in. But "just selling"—especially when that means (as it often does) more pitching, presenting, and closing—doesn't work the way it once did. Fifty years ago, companies' balance sheets depended on physical inventory—products a customer could touch. Those products could be distinguished by a unique feature or benefit that might stand out in the market for decades. Today, so much is intangible and ephemeral, and nothing is unique for long. Companies have run with the outdated assumption that their competitive advantage is contained only in the function of their products and services, the bells and whistles of their "unique" solution—what they sell. But uniqueness is just as ephemeral as intellectual property.

You rarely have to persuade a CEO of the importance of innovation. Most naturally love to be associated with the shiny new thing. They want to make and sell something different or, even better, make and sell something that stands out in the market. But no *thing* stands out for long. No single innovation can ever provide a long-term competitive advantage. Fast followers in every industry are getting faster all the time. Think of Blockbuster, BlackBerry, and MySpace, which were all unique in their time. Now think of the fast followers that overtook them. Their names are legion. If you manage to earn strong margins on your newest, most innovative products, services, or capabilities, you can bet the bliss won't last long. Before you know it, your advantage is weakened by a competitor with a similar, better, or cheaper offering.

When the iPhone debuted in 2007, there was nothing else like it in the world. The touchscreen, the apps, the web browser, and a slew of other features made it totally unique, hailed by many as one of the greatest inventions of the last fifty years. And if you wanted this package, you could only get it from Apple, and the exclusive service provider was AT&T.

But within a mere thirty-six months, at least two dozen competing devices emerged from a variety of manufacturers, with service offered by every major carrier. Competition is inevitable. Today, there is still only one iPhone, and it is still a market leader, but a multitude of other options are available for consumers—most of them pretty terrific too. Apple's uniqueness vanished more quickly than it takes to pay off a car—and this was for one of the most innovative products ever. Apple quickly went from a position of uniqueness in *what* they sell to a commoditized market.

In today's markets, the half-life of differentiation is notoriously brief. Competition can replicate and leapfrog you faster than ever before. In the eyes of customers, products start to look pretty much the same. Commoditization is a marketplace pandemic, and how good your stuff is no longer has compelling—let alone sovereign or unique—differentiating relevance. All the players are now obliged to continually innovate.

But there is an additional route to a competitive edge. Apple has always excelled in innovating what they sell, but they have also been extremely good at how they sell it and who they sell it to. Customers are an eternal need; no matter how unique your offering, you need someone to buy it. In recent years, business leadership at every level has been talking about the customer experience and how to create genuine value for the right customer. The topic has even earned its own acronym, CX, and it deserves it. Leaders are right to focus on it. What part of your company is best positioned to create that value? Who in your organization connects directly, daily, constantly to the customer? One CEO told researchers, "I typically do not see customers. That's what the sales force is for."[3] The customer journey starts with the sales experience. To guide that journey, that sales experience needs to be central to your goals. Your company is in a conversation with the customer on every sales call. The sales team is delivering a message—whether that message is your intended one or not.

The job of the contemporary sales organization is not to sell a product or service or even a solution. It is to design and deliver a compelling and differentiating sales experience. Done well, and done consistently, it will produce profitable revenue. But it is not enough to say that revenue and even profit or customer loyalty result only from high-performing sellers. Revenue and profit come from the people in your company who interact with customers—specialists who offer the most compelling experience. For the customer, that doesn't mean a product. It doesn't mean explaining a list of features or the generic benefits of a product or service. It means a solution to their specific problem or helping them to achieve an objective. It means using expertise to explore issues and helping them to see issues differently. Identifying, diagnosing, surfacing, and then finding ways to address the customer's problem will not only generate revenue but will win the company far more than its fair share of revenue in a given market. It leaps beyond transactional revenue to expand margins and create profit streams.

While those are the major themes that have been commonly understood for consultative selling and solution sales for decades now, it is still not common practice. Sales organizations, lacking effective strategic leadership, continue to underperform at creating a memorable sales experience.

The next step beyond innovation—and maybe the last step for a company's intellectual property to become a competitive advantage—is the sales experience. Sales professionals offering customer-centric value draw those customers to you and give them an additional reason to choose your company. That reason, when all other factors are similar in the eyes of the customer, will tip the scales in your favor. The competitive edge belongs to companies that use their sales organization to add and even create value, not merely to convey it. The leaders of these companies have learned to make *how* they sell, not just *what* they sell, integral to their overall business strategy. In those companies, sales is the execution of that strategy, not a sidebar to it. Sales is the direct connection between what you want your company to be and the customer. Sales must live that strategy on every call, but they can only do that if you lead them.

The Butterfly Effect

In 1972, MIT professor and meteorologist Edward Lorenz presented at a meeting of the American Association for the Advancement of Science. His talk was titled "Predictability: Does the Flap of a Butterfly's Wings in Brazil Set Off a Tornado in Texas?"[1] One day, I ran across the paper he published after the talk and had an epiphany. I had certainly heard about the butterfly effect before, as you may have as well, but the business implications had never been clear before.

The idea is this: a butterfly flapping its wings in Brazil creates perturbations in the surrounding air that set off a chain of atmospheric events. Weeks later, those minuscule fluctuations influence the formation of a tornado in Texas. Lorenz was working on an algorithm to analyze the effects of atmospheric phenomena on weather. He wanted to more accurately predict weather conditions. He wrote a computer program in which he applied his algorithm to known historical weather data, using that data to forecast weather that had already happened. This allowed him to assess the accuracy of the algorithm.

Lorenz predicted sunshine in a certain location on a certain day. Then he looked at what had actually happened in that place and on that day: rain. Disappointed, Lorenz meticulously backtracked through his work, intent on finding his wrong turn. He reran the program and got the same wrong result, a prediction of sunshine totally at odds with the historical fact of stormy weather.

Nothing about the algorithm or the software seemed wrong, but Lorenz questioned one of the practical decisions he had made. Back in 1972, computing power was ridiculously puny compared to what we have today. So, to save precious memory, processor power, and computational time, Lorenz performed all his calculations to the thousandth decimal place—0.001—and no further. Calculating to more than three decimal places seemed to him wasteful overkill.

But then Lorenz realized that this limitation, which he considered obvious, was the one untested assumption he had made. So, he decided to test it. Lorenz rewrote his software to calculate the same data to the ten thousandth (0.0001) and then to the hundred thousandth (0.00001) decimal place. With this last iteration, putting five digits to the right of the decimal point, the algorithm finally predicted rain. The forecast it produced coincided with reality.

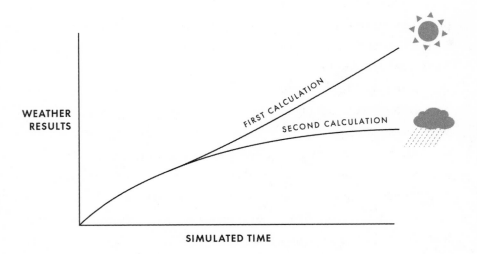

I had the nagging feeling that I had seen this movie before. When I saw a chart illustrating Lorenz's point, I suddenly realized why it was so familiar. My clients had shown me such charts many, many times.

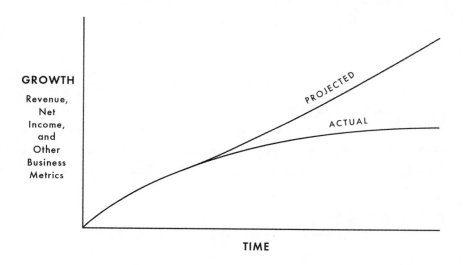

I had seen many sunny revenue forecasts end in stormy weather at the conclusion of the quarter or the year. I had—many times—listened to executives argue with one another about how wrong their forecasts turned out to be. In business, the real problems begin when the expectation and reality are misaligned. When targets are missed, when deadlines continue to slip, when results do not meet expectations (even if those expectations were based on unrealistic hopes), the missed expectations cascade into negative consequences that can range from disappointing investors and owners and a declining stock price to leaders losing jobs. Leaders are hired to grow their organizations. If they fail, the consequences roll through the entire organization—missed bonuses, budget cuts, layoffs, and so on. And because of these consequences, missed expectations propel executives to identify the problem that led to poor performance and address it.

POINTING THE FINGER

The jolt of shattered expectations triggers finger pointing. What went wrong? Leadership rarely looks at more than a few decimal points and often stops at the most plausible—or seemingly obvious—answer. In the case of revenue growth projections that don't pan out, the easiest plausible explanation is that sales dropped the ball. Sales, after all, is the function most obviously connected to revenue, right? It is human nature to blame a bad outcome on the actor closest to that outcome. It is just plausible enough that executives rarely consider deepening their analysis, and they rarely include more decimal places, as Lorenz did. That kind of increased precision might cause the finger to point upstream in the organization. The critical missteps that resulted in a disappointing quarter might have come from the executives' own actions and decisions, which are comparable to Lorenz's inputs—his calculations and the number of decimal points he used in those calculations.

Don't get me wrong. The sellers and sales management are the ones who turned in the disappointing numbers. They are certainly an important factor in the equation. But just as stopping at three decimal places failed to produce an accurate weather forecast, pinning the rap on sales may produce a plausible answer but not necessarily the complete truth. When corporate revenue growth aspirations go wrong, the cause, if you really search for it, is frequently found in the C-suite.

Sellers make the kind of sales they are led and managed to make. If they are led and managed to sell whatever they can to whoever will buy it now—and are hired, trained, compensated, and rewarded only for transactions—then they will do exactly that. But they'll seek out the easy win, not the strategic one. If the people on your sales team aren't recognized as a critical part of the execution of your go-to-market strategy, you shouldn't be surprised when they ignore it—if they even understand it. If they are told to sell solutions and to be consultative but aren't led, managed, and evaluated that way, if they are systematically encouraged to simply repeat the "selling points" of your product like a living brochure, they will never provide a high-value sales experience for your customers. How could they?

Sales executives, sales managers, and sellers cannot succeed in executing the company strategy on their own. Sometimes the failure stems from a bad decision. Even more often, however, it stems from the absence of quality input. If an organization does not start with a sufficiently detailed growth strategy, the entire system will lack the guidance needed to achieve the correct growth and results, in the same way that Lorenz's calculations lacked sufficient decimal points to achieve the correct weather prediction. A sales organization capable of creating, not merely conveying, value can function only in a growth-focused company culture that establishes a direct working connection from the C-suite to sales, linking all the functions in between. The farther up the organization chart an input (a decision, action, or communication) is made, the greater its impact on the output of growth. Remember: A small action early in the process (like a butterfly flapping its wings or strategy decisions in the C-suite) can lead to enormous outcomes down the road (a tornado or phenomenal growth). Actions and decisions must begin at the top, where all the strategic inputs are formulated. It must begin with you as a Growth Leader.

Unplugged from the company strategy, the sellers' best efforts will too often fall short—far short—of what is needed to produce sustained strategic growth. Without C-level engagement with the sales organization to both enable and require a more strategic approach to selling, the sellers will sell the best way they know how, but with unpredictable or suboptimal results.

FROM CHAOS TO INTENTION

The purpose of any strategy is to replace that unpredictability with intentionality. The goal is to take the right actions early to ensure the outcomes you want and not simply hope for the desired outcomes as the fallout of accidental leadership. The impact of the strategies, perspectives, words, actions, and decisions of the leadership team compound as they filter through layers of management to the rest of the organization. This has an acute effect on the sales team as they execute your strategy in the market. As the top leadership, you need to appreciate that all your decisions and actions—good, bad, carefully calculated, or downright thoughtless—impact all aspects of your company's performance. The sales organization is simply an extension of the company's strategy.

Leaders who have realized this and have embraced strategic growth as their own responsibility are distinctly in the minority. Most executives voice their approval of ambitious priorities and organizational change or even transformation, but few are prepared to actually drive that change. And a huge part of leading success is driving the execution of your business strategy through every aspect of the business, including the sales function. But today, only a fraction of executives reap the massive advantage of a sales team that is directly wired into the priorities of top leadership.

Few leaders use the sales organization for what it could be: a way to differentiate their company's offerings from their competitors'. It's little wonder, since building a high-performance sales organization staffed by professionals who add value through expertise and insight is considerably harder than hiring talking brochures and quantifying their success using short-term quotas to generate immediate results. To be truly effective, the sales team must be an integral part of the enterprise's growth-focused strategy. And that growth focus requires leaders who drive strategic engagement with every function in the organization.

You've surely heard this notion about the importance of alignment before; thought leaders have been harping on it for years. There are two reasons we're still talking about it. First, it works. If it didn't, it would have gone the way of rotary phones and VHS rentals. Second, *leaders aren't listening*. That gives you—the reader of this book—an immediate competitive advantage over the 86 percent of leaders who are ignoring all that conversation about alignment with their sales organization.

A company's success, as measured by some form of growth, begins with the aspiration we call *strategy*. The degree of certainty—of intentionality—we can give this aspiration is determined solely by effective organizational leadership. My goal is to inform and empower you and your company. I want to help you engage with your entire organization intentionally and strategically to differentiate, cultivate customer loyalty, and grow. I want to enable you to realize more opportunities for growth with strategy so finely focused and intentionally executed that you are best described as a Growth Leader.

WHAT TO DO ABOUT IT

How do you become a Growth Leader? Should you go out and recruit better sales managers? Should you enroll your sales team in the latest sales training system? Should you create a new incentive plan? Well, no. It's not that any of these options are bad. But you've likely already tried them, and it hasn't gotten you the results you want. The problem is not simply your salespeople or their training or compensation. The problem is cultural.

If your revenues are driven by a sales organization, then the center of that drive—sales—should be at the heart of your company's strategy. This means your salespeople, who interact directly with your customers as part of their core function, need to fully understand your strategy. They must be encouraged, managed, rewarded, and even required to pursue broader goals to achieve the profitable revenue growth your business needs. Cultivating and supporting such a sales organization is an executive leadership job and requires a systematic change of mindset from the top down. This mindset shift must be a cultural imperative throughout the company. For your employees—in every department, not just sales—to embody your strategy, you must consistently communicate it to them and inspire them to embrace it. If you do not connect every person in your company to a specific goal and a path to achieve it, your strategy is just empty words. You are the only one who can lead this level of organizational alignment.

I have written about leadership in two other books and numerous articles for *Harvard Business Review*, *Forbes*, and other periodicals. This book is different. It is based on observing and researching the intersection of organizational leadership, strategy, and sales. In addition to my own research, I have commissioned work from Amy Humble and Sue Barlow, who both served for years in leadership roles with Jim Collins's Good to Great Project. They helped me with research focused on how organizational leaders integrate the sales organization into their strategic plan and why those leaders so often fail to do so. This book incorporates quotations on these topics from our interviews with CEOs and other executives. The purpose of my work has always been to supply my clients with something most of them lack: a robust, fully functioning link between the C-suite and the sales organization that creates a powerful competitive advantage.

START FLAPPING

Edward Lorenz sought the truth by tracking it up the chain of causation. He discovered that small initial differences—some of them invisible until you get to the one-hundred-thousandth decimal place—could trigger large, unexpected changes downstream. A seemingly insignificant input, such as the flapping of a butterfly's wings, can eventually affect something as momentous as a tornado.

Although we know this as the butterfly effect, it is also known as "a sensitive dependence on initial conditions." Time after time in my consulting work, I have been struck by just how sensitive the system of a company is to the initial conditions created by the CEO and other top-level executives. Look far enough upstream through your company's systems and structure, tracing outcomes to initial inputs, and you will find not *chaos* but *cause*. The priorities and goals that drive the company—the bad, the ugly, and also the good—don't just appear out of nowhere. The leaders' directives multiply, ramify, and amplify throughout the business, for good or ill. Poor sales performance is usually evidence of a sales organization held (intentionally or not) at a stiff arm's length from the C-suite or even utterly disconnected from it. Without actively forging a link between strategy and sales, the C-suite may predict sunshine and instead wind up with a very soggy parade.

One way or another, business growth is not just the goal but the responsibility of all CEOs. But it is not enough for the CEO to command the company's sellers to sally forth to win customers and raise revenue. Lorenz's example of chaos—unpredictability—shows us that the path to revenue growth and margin expansion is more complex than a simple command-and-execute sequence. The patterns can be traced back to initial inputs (executive decisions and actions), which, like the flapping of a butterfly wing, have an outsized impact on the output. To create a tornado of growth, you have to flap your wings.

CHAPTER 1

The Hidden Differentiator

Many CEOs have told me and my research team that the sales organization is always *naturally* more distant from the C-suite than many other functions. But the sales function is also closest to the *customer*. They speak to customers every day, on every call. If you accept the natural distance between sales and leadership, you also admit a huge—and costly—distance between leadership and customers.

Business is not about leaving things in their natural state. It is about making them better. Being a Growth Leader means being an executive who relentlessly dares to challenge the natural state of the organization by creating strategic connections at every level. That means closer ties to your leaders of sales and to the company's actual customers. The sales experience can directly link your corporate strategy with your ideal customer to provide solutions for their specific needs. By overcoming that natural distance, you uncover a powerful hidden differentiator.

THE CUSTOMER EXPERIENCE
IS THE SALES EXPERIENCE

Senior executives build strategies for growth that include developing new products and services through research and development, integrating offerings, or acquiring other firms. But they often forget that the success or failure of their strategy is determined by each individual sales call. Every sales call represents one moment where the core elements of a strategy are executed in real time. For many organizations, such execution happens hundreds—even thousands—of times each day. For the business, this can become either a massive accumulation of wins or death by a thousand cuts.

For obvious reasons, frontline sales and customer-contact professionals are literally in a position to directly impact revenue dramatically. They not only influence how much customers buy from the company but whether they buy anything at all. A McKinsey & Company analysis of buying behavior among 1,200 B2B purchasers revealed that, on average, 25 percent of the purchasing decision is determined by the "overall sales experience."[1] This is surely much too big to be dismissed as a statistical artifact. A 25 percent edge is a differentiator in any marketplace, right?

IMPORTANCE OF SALES EXPERIENCE TO PURCHASING DECISION: PERCENT

CUSTOMER
SURVEYS

ACTUAL
IMPORTANCE

PRODUCT/SERVICE FEATURES   PRICE   SERVICE/SUPPORT   RELIABILITY   OVERALL SALES EXPERIENCE

Figure produced with data from the McKinsey & Company survey of 1,200 B2B purchasers

The research generated another interesting point. In the original survey data, the sales experience was the least important category. But the researchers went further, understanding that you should never trust the data in a self-survey on its own. When they analyzed the actual buying behaviors of those same B2B purchasers and correlated their decisions with supplier performance, the sales experience was more than three times more important than stated. How customers answer questions on a survey can be very different from their actual behaviors. Many customers will suggest that price, support, or other factors are more important to them than the sales experience, but their actions indicate a different story.[2] This also sheds some light on why the sales experience hasn't been prioritized as a differentiator by many executives: It's not straightforwardly expressed by customers as a decision criterion. But it is one. A powerful one.

Even more remarkably, a survey of B2B customers by Gartner[3] revealed that, among existing customers, the buyer's experience during the sales process accounted for 53 percent of the purchasing decision. That's more than the brand, delivery, and the product itself combined.

What executive would not give their eyeteeth for an advantage that can help their company win 25 to 53 percent of the customer decision criteria? This is a huge competitive advantage. Yet, for most companies, it lies fallow at worst and is underleveraged at best. The headline here is also the bottom line: The sales experience is a powerfully differentiating decision criterion that is routinely overlooked or dismissed outright. The sales experience differentiates your company. It can be a deciding factor in winning in the market. Or it can hurt you and even cause you to lose the market.

Given this choice, what executive would *not* make moves to claim the advantage? But when I ask top leaders to enumerate their competitive advantages, the sales experience never shows up. It rarely registers with executives. When I ask them about their competitive strategy, the sales experience is missing in action there, too. Leaders readily mention brand, quality, price, and service. And even though the effect of a positive sales experience can rival or even dwarf the effects of those other factors, it is conspicuously absent from the strategy of most companies. If you are competitive in your brand, price, and service *and* you have a great sales experience, you will win more than your fair share of business.

The customer experience is so central that it has spawned dozens of conferences, associations, and the like. I have never encountered a C-suite leader who denies the importance of CX, but a briefing paper for Harvard Business Review Analytic Services claims that just 46 percent of executives think "revenue leaders"—including sales leaders—"will play a role in their organization's CX strategy."[4] The problem is that most of the CX efforts are all about what happens *after* the customer has made a purchase. This is too late. As I said in an interview in that same paper, the sales experience is the first mile of the CX highway. If it's a bad experience, customers get off at exit 1, and there is no CX, no revenues at all.[5]

But the sales experience is rarely talked about as a critical driver of the CX even though they are essentially the same thing, at least in the early stages of a customer relationship. Your salesperson is your customer's connection to your company. They're the first point of contact. And they may be the only one if the customer does not perceive value in the relationship. Done right, the sales experience is a powerful differentiator.

Over the long term, the sales experience is essential to growth. It roots your strategy in the dynamic realities of your marketplace, your industry, and the technological and economic environments. As CEO of Avnet, Bill Amelio recalled for my research team what happened in 2016, when the Fortune 500 company faced an existential crisis. Avnet had struggled in that fiscal year, with sales falling 6.1 percent and net income sliding 11.4 percent. This drop brought the company to the very brink of disaster, and Amelio was hired with a mandate to "accelerate growth, drive a greater sense of urgency and enhance the company's focus on execution." Amelio himself said that the company needed to "leverage its strength around sales, operations, and vendor- and solution-provider relationships."[6]

"The only reason we are still in existence," Amelio told my research team, "is because of our sales department. The relationships our sales team had with our customers kept us alive." His sales team sold strategically, focusing on how they could help customers achieve their objectives and promoting the value Avnet represented *for its customers*. The last thing those customers wanted was for the partner they so highly valued to go out of business. For that reason, they stayed with Avnet as it worked to solve its supplier problems. If you create a compelling strategy and a sales experience to sell it, your customers won't just buy your products and services; they may end up saving your company. By September 2016, Avnet's stock had stabilized, and the company was back on track.[7]

SELL DIFFERENTLY

Whatever term we use—*consultative selling, solution selling*, or other terms that emerge as descriptions for a value-focused approach—we are really talking about one thing: the sales experience. It is an indisputable point of differentiation that should impact strategy. Inside every company is an urgent—if mostly unacknowledged—need not only to sell different things, but to sell things differently. A consultative sales experience generates insight into the customer's challenges and helps them see issues and solutions they had not considered. It goes beyond a product to a deeper solution. In fact, most products or services are not a solution until they are connected to problems the customer needs to solve or objectives the customer wants to achieve. It's that connection that turns whatever you provide into a solution. The sales experience identifies that solution and connects the customer to it.

Recently, Gartner forecasted that the market for a particular technology sector, the Internet of Things (IoT), would grow exponentially into the trillions of dollars.[8] The technology exists in abundance, so innovation is prolific and, therefore, there are many *different things* to sell. But most companies still lag behind the opportunity. There is not yet a clear-cut market leader that manages to sell things *differently*. Even companies in some of the most highly innovative industries—such as the burgeoning realm of

IoT itself—fail to imbue the sales experience with the value that a problem-solving consultative approach provides. A multitrillion-dollar market has no single market leader because no one has successfully adopted a concept that has been a common and acknowledged approach for more than forty years.

The industry sector is, of course, not the point here. What is vital to recognize is that a massive opportunity for winning in the market is hiding in plain sight. To gain this competitive advantage, you must take the sales experience as seriously as the products and services you provide.

In *Rethinking the Sales Force*, Neil Rackham and John De Vincentis wrote that the purpose of a sales force must now shift from *communicating* value to *creating* it. He quotes Burleigh Hutchins, the late chairman of Zymark, a provider of laboratory automation: "A segment of your customers [is] buying your advice more than your product. They need you to invest in understanding their business, and they'll make the investment required to educate you . . . They want to spend time with you. You'd better be prepared to do it, or a competitor will give them the kind of hand-holding they need. It doesn't matter if you've a better product. You can't afford to be too busy to spend the time it takes."[9]

It is no longer sufficient to deploy a strategy that has the sales force focused on pitching, presenting, and closing. There is too little in that approach to be useful. Today, there must be something more if a company wants to differentiate on something more than price. The sales experience itself must create that differentiating value. That value is what tips the business in your favor when all other things like features, price, and brand are similar or identical in the eyes of customers and the market.

Today, sellers must provide value that buyers cannot get simply by surfing the web or doing more focused research online or elsewhere. Such value will never be created simply by sending your salespeople to another training program, any more than a few days at a golf camp will turn a weekend golfer into a pro. Don't get me wrong. Many training programs are worthwhile, and I'd even suggest they are necessary at some level. They can improve the technique and skill required in the consultative sale. But they aren't sufficient to capitalize on the opportunity to design and execute a sales experience that creates value and differentiates your business in the market. That requires more. It calls for a strategic shift at the executive level.

SALES CALLS YOUR CUSTOMERS WOULD PAY FOR

Sales does not need to be told to sell or sell more. It is implied in the job. But often, it is the only primary direction they are given by leadership. What they need is clear direction about their role in creating value and how they can execute in a way that differentiates your business. They need clarity about what kind of business to pursue within your target markets and, equally as important, what to stay away from because it's not a good match even if they could get a deal. Communicating this vision is key to ensuring that the sales team is effectively executing your strategy in the market, and it requires that you have a voice with the sales organization. This does not mean that the CEO or any other executives should micromanage the salesforce. But the leadership message should be a mandate for your sales leadership to focus on customer value and to design sales processes that mirror the process by which buyers buy. Be clear in your definition of what constitutes the value that sales professionals should strive to bring to the sales experience.

As I wrote in an article for *Harvard Business Review*, you can solve this with the basic economic equation for value: $V = B - C$: Value equals benefits minus cost. Then follow the logic of that equation by asking yourself what my former boss and sales guru Neil Rackham asks: "Would your customer write you a check for the sales call?" Instead of telling sellers what they already know—sell stuff and lots of it—the CEO should ask them Rackham's question.

If the candid answer is no, then leadership and sales have to understand that the sales function isn't providing much—if any—additional value and doesn't justify the cost of being there. If there's not much value in its sales calls, why would a company invest significantly in the go-to-market approach? And if customers don't find enough value in the sales experience, they'll look for ways to avoid it, to minimize it, or to eliminate it altogether by buying online or from a competitor.

If, on the other hand, the seller is delivering a sales call valuable enough to customers that they would, in fact, pay for it, this becomes a recurring source of revenue. It brings the customer back for more. They will be more willing to pay your higher fees, will be less contentious in price negotiations, and will show greater loyalty.

This form of truly valuable sales call is less common, but when you experience it as a customer, it stays with you. Inspired by my own experience of living in a hot place, Florida, and having an old house that stubbornly resisted all efforts to air-condition it adequately, I brought in three firms to advise me. The first two offered to sell me exactly what I suggested to them I needed: a larger system to pump more air through the house. They both proposed the same larger brand-name unit, and both recited the same technical specs like SEER ratings, energy efficiency ratios, and Btus per hour. Each came with the same installation process. I figured I'd negotiate to the least expensive option, as they both seemed good.

The third seller was different. The salesperson—I even remember his name: Garry—took time to study my house, measuring the heat load from large windows and the placement and routing of the airflow with my current ductwork. He was able to identify issues that I hadn't given much thought to. And because of the diagnostic process, he was able to make a detailed recommendation that I hadn't considered. It was an out-of-the-box solution. In fact, it was out of two boxes. He explained that, because of the design of my house, I needed two air-conditioning units, each assigned to a different floor. He further explained that the current ductwork would require reconfiguration because of the inefficiency of the airflow. This turned out to be an issue that would have prevented any amount of AC unit strength from producing satisfactory results, even if I had bought the other larger AC system. Garry persuaded me not with a pitch about product specs but by taking the time to understand the uniqueness of my old home and by using his expertise to form a solution I would not have come up with on my own. Garry's experience and expertise—not the new AC units—provided a better way to cool my home.

Not coincidentally, all of the equipment Garry sold me in the process was available to the first two reps I met. They were all distributors of the same major brands, but Garry's approach made all the difference. I did pay more—two AC units cost more than one, and the installation was considerably more involved—but what I really paid for was this particular sales experience, which solved my problem. That sales call enabled me to make the best decision, and I have never regretted it—despite it costing 300 percent more than the other options. Had I yielded to one of the first two pitches, I would have been sweaty and miserable and full of regret. And I have remained loyal for the last fifteen years in the face of considerable competition.

To create truly valuable sales calls, your sales team, much like my AC expert, must move away from transactional interactions and toward consultative relationships. Here are a few ways to do that:

Help your customers with problems they don't see

The best sales organizations I've worked with do an extraordinary job of focusing on finding problems the customer didn't know they had and then helping the customer solve them. They have a sales process that is based on a mutual diagnosis. The sellers lead discussions about the client's business, looking for problems in need of solutions their company offers. You can see how your sales team must be knowledgeable about the full scope of your strategic offerings—not just the latest product—to be able to diagnose these issues.

Help your customers with problems they don't know are problems

Clients frequently tell me that they greatly value the ability of their sales reps to help them make a case for change. Sales reps do that by helping their customers see the effect of a problem on the organization. A customer may be aware of an issue—say, a morale problem—but may not yet see the effect it may have down the line. They might have only a bit of employee turnover at the moment, but a serious morale issue could damage recruitment and productivity and snowball into a much bigger issue. The seller and buyer discuss the implications for the business and identify a solution together.

Help your customer see hidden opportunities

Although your customers' problems—or *pain points*—are an important opportunity, great sales teams also know there's value in finding and exploiting successes. Creating value in the sales process is about raising the bar just as much as it is about solving problems. Discovering these untapped opportunities with the customer opens the way for great value creation by your sales team. And discussing them together through back-and-forth conversation makes it less likely that a client will react defensively to something they perhaps should have already known. They may be more likely to embrace both the opportunities and the messenger who helped to uncover them.

Help your customers find solutions they haven't considered

When your best sellers discuss your company's offerings, they present them not as a series of features and benefits but as solutions that address the expressed needs of the client. The key to creating value is to do so in a way that the client has not considered. Few customers will know everything your product or service can do, so finding a way to uniquely address their expressed need is both possible and powerful.

Help your customers connect with additional resources

Your company—and your sales team—can't solve every problem. Not every customer will be a good match with what you offer right now. But that doesn't mean that you can't help them. Your team can create additional value by connecting the customer with others in your organization or even referring them to outside experts who can help them through their specific issue. Your team will have helped the customer, and that will help you build loyalty and customer trust, which usually leads to more business.

Selling is not about pushing a product or service or calling whatever you sell a solution. It is about improving your customer's situation—preferably but not necessarily with your products and services. Companies who help buyers find real value through the selling process sell more and command a premium for their offerings. Here is an example of that mindset in action:

The Commercial Aviation Solutions (CAS) group within Fortune 500 defense contractor L3Harris was on the verge of a transformation. A leader in the design and manufacture of flight simulators, avionics, and training solutions, they had made several acquisitions that would now enable them to put data analytics at the core of what they offered.

Alan Crawford, president of L3Harris CAS, told me:

> I knew when we put data analytics [DA] services at the core of our strategy that we'd need to focus on two things. The first was obvious. We needed to complete the build-out of technical capabilities to automate our analysis and be able to do it all over the world. But the second would be the key to our expansion. That was to improve our ability to sell the business outcomes that DA produces at the executive level.
>
> If we were going to sell our DA capabilities, it would have to be to a different level of customer than we'd traditionally deal with. Not someone in procurement or flight operations that was looking to buy flight data recorders, surveillance systems, flight simulators, and training. Our DA solutions need to be sold to senior leaders using our insights and expertise to help them capitalize on opportunities to achieve their goals—improved safety, financial improvements, avoidance of incidents, improving on-time delivery, reducing waste, cutting

emissions, etc. Selling these solutions would require us to take a new approach to the sales experience and make it a vital part of our strategy to win a different kind of business.

If this approach was new to the sales organization, it was also new to the customers. "Some of the solutions we were looking to sell were new and difficult for our customers to define."

I worked with Alan and his executive leadership team to drive this shift in the strategy for their business. It would require not only selling different things but selling differently. Like many companies today, they are moving from selling their conventional products to selling a broader and more valuable solution set.

As Robin Glover-Faure, senior vice president of L3Harris CAS, explains, "We sell two categories of product: avionics products, such as flight recorders and data collection devices, and training solutions. Our sales team sells the whole portfolio. [They] are pretty accomplished at what you might describe as conventional product selling." But they'd like to focus on a third tier of product: analyzing the data from those avionics devices. "The data analytics is the growth area of our business. Our vision is that data analytics will actually be at the heart of our full product portfolio."

Robin explains that the company's products produce a lot of data.

> What we want to do is extract that data with the airlines to create a data pool that can be mined to provide insights for the customer. These can be in terms of how their aircraft are being operated in terms of efficiencies—for example, the amount of energy that the aircraft is using during an approach. It could also be on the training side, where we could provide insights on how, for example, we could make training more effective.

Early in our engagement, I laid out for Alan and Robin the notion of the sales experience as a central part of the strategy and the importance of creating a sales call your customers would pay for. This, in fact, is what they wanted for the sales organization; they recognized that the need to sell solutions at the executive level would require this. Robin described their goal as having "such a rich conversation with a customer that they actually want to have the conversation because you are going to provide the pathway for them that gives them a data solution that is going to effectively help them meet their goal."

Robin explains that "many chief operating officers of airlines at the moment are focused on sustainability goals. Is their airline making progress against the declared emissions goals for 2050? When the COO reports to the board, does he or she have the data that shows the changes that are being made to the operation and to training that are making progress toward those sustainabilities?" The sales organization needed to pivot to consultatively selling these solutions. They needed to lead discussions with customers that helped them to see that "we're going to give you the tools, and we're going to give you the insight for you to be able to achieve your goals."

Creating value, for CAS, speaks directly to how sales can craft a sales experience that will help customers see unique ways to leverage the data analytics product to avoid risk and optimize operations. This, in turn, will drive successful execution of the business transformation L3 Harris CAS is seeking—to put its data analytics capability at the very center of its long-established business in avionics, flight recorder technology, and training tools. These products *measure* performance. Data analytics would enable airline operators to transform *measurement* into *improvement* across flight operations, training, scheduling, maintenance, and so on. Data analytics, as the heart of its business, would be a powerful differentiator for the company. This required creating a sales experience that would be, as President Alan Crawford put it, "a vital differentiator . . . key to driving adoption of our services. The executives who buy our solutions become our partners through the sales experience."

FROM TRANSACTION TO PARTNERSHIP

Companies such as L3Harris stand in contrast to companies that do not achieve growth driven by strategy. This does not mean that they lack a strategy, but it does mean that they have a leadership disconnect between top executives and sales. That disconnect is often epitomized by the assumption that sales is merely a series of transactions. But growth is more than the product of opportunistic transactions. It is the result of strong relationships built with customers whose needs you meet, problems you solve, horizons you broaden, opportunities you multiply, and expectations you exceed. Many executives are conversant enough to talk about this. But few do the work of connecting sales with strategy and leading the alignment effort in earnest.

Transactional revenue is nothing to sneeze at. But it is not enough. Successful companies are built on the strategic investments of the entire organization. Both sales and company leadership must understand the strategic value of the data sales collects from customers, and this data must be used to determine and tune a coherent strategy. Only in this way can growth be made both efficient and scalable. Top executives who take a hands-off approach to sales and customers may drive their sales leaders and sellers just as hard as Growth Leaders do. But by demanding that they generate revenue by making sales rather than executing the corporate strategy, differentiating with value, and creating relationships, the company's leaders drive salespeople along a narrow road with a restrictive speed limit.

The great unrealized opportunity for growth is in your sales team; sales is more often than not an underleveraged asset, a hidden differentiator. Top leadership needs to demand more from the sales organization. Sure, the C-suite is not shy in its expectation that sales make its numbers, but I'm not talking about mere targets and goals. Growth-minded executives understand that truly significant growth is an issue that involves the entire company and, therefore, is first and foremost a leadership issue.

The sales organization should not be asked merely to *sell* value. It should be strategically engaged in *creating* it. Top leadership must begin thinking about sales in this way—as critical to the creation of value. This means that the sales organization must be positioned within the company to deliver those sales calls your customers would willingly pay for. The value proposition created by the sales team does not reside in the product or service alone but in the company's value to the customer as a helpful, even indispensable, partner. Deliver this level of sales experience and the value of the sale scales up and becomes a collaborative relationship cocreated by the seller and the customer.

Bill Amelio, while at Avnet, did not have to be persuaded of the value of his sales organization. The relationships they created were lifesavers. Little wonder, then, that he champions listening to sales reps and customers when creating strategy. "As far as determining what strategic markets sales should target, my strategy is to listen to what the field has to say, then make adjustments." Moreover, he understands that for the entire organization to value sales, that sentiment must come from the top. "When the CEO values sales," he told us, "then everyone else values sales."

The sales experience is the opening move in the customer experience. Without the sales experience, there is no customer experience. Without a sales experience that executes strategy, the right customers will have a difficult time seeing what differentiates your company from your competitors. Fail to seize that opportunity and you retain few levers to control the customer's buying decision. The most overused lever is price, and moving that lever means sacrificing your margin.

THE SALES EXPERIENCE IS THE CUSTOMER EXPERIENCE

Selling highly differentiated products, services, and capabilities almost always benefits from a great sales experience that executes the company strategy in every sales call. As we have seen, a great sales experience increases your likelihood of gaining a 25 percent edge in winning a new customer's buying decision, and that number more than doubles for returning customers.

Sales leaders and managers cannot shoulder the ultimate responsibility of generating revenue. Even in the case of sales organizations that sell minimally differentiated commodified products, failing to empower and require the sales professionals to deliver a strategically aligned sales experience can be an act of self-sabotage. The advance of strategy to execution cannot occur in internal meetings, reviews, and reporting. It is all in the sales process, which culminates in the sales experience. The goal is for the sales organization to understand that effective execution requires bringing the go-to-market strategy to life in every sales call. In order to truly understand that, they must be recruited, hired, compensated, developed, and led to enact that strategy.

Capturing a quarter to a half of the buying decision requires corporate leadership that aligns the strategy with the entire company—especially the sales organization. It calls for leadership to ensure that the company's sales professionals deliver a sales experience so valuable that customers say they would be willing to pay a premium for what you offer. They will see your company as worth doing business with because each touchpoint in the sales process provides rich insight and relevant expertise that enables them to achieve their objectives. Such a sales process helps them solve the problems they know they have. It helps them identify problems they are unaware of. It opens their minds to opportunities not previously considered. Your company's sales process prompts them to think differently about solutions that will help them get where they need to be. It makes them think differently about you and your company.

DO YOU EVEN KNOW YOUR STRATEGY?

One huge impediment is almost certainly keeping you from bringing your strategy to life: no one knows what it is. Ask anyone in your organization to explain the company's strategy in the most basic terms. The odds are they cannot even begin to do so. At best, they may come up with some version of a mission statement or a vision statement—the destination with no map to get there.

Collis and Rukstad established *objective*, *scope*, and *advantage* as the mandatory dimensions of any strategy in their classic *Harvard Business Review* article. The title of the piece, "Can You Say What Your Strategy Is?," was the gist of the question they asked a large cross section of executives.[10] It turns out that most of the respondents couldn't—at least not with crisp clarity. This may be shocking, but it isn't surprising.

I wasn't surprised by it, because in my work, I frequently ask leaders this very question: "Tell me about your strategy?" I end up listening, usually for much too long. In that time, the CEO's description has lost any of the thrust, sense, or cogency needed in a strategic framework; its meaning gets muddy and then is lost.

A McKinsey survey of 772 directors revealed that only 34 percent believed that their corporate boards understood their firm's strategy. Other surveys show that, in most firms, fewer than half of the employees say they understand their firm's strategy. And sales teams seem to be disproportionately affected. Sellers rate their own understanding of company strategy far lower than the leaders rate *their* understanding—which is already rather low. True, the C-suite believes strategy has fairly little influence on what the sales team does, but the sales team's estimation of the impact of strategy is even lower. Vanishingly low, in fact. The closer employees get to the customer— and none get closer than sales professionals—the less they understand the company's strategy.[11]

When I speak at conferences and company meetings, I often ask top corporate leadership and their sales teams two questions:

- On a scale of 1 to 10, how well does your sales team understand your strategy?

- On a scale of 1 to 10, how much does your strategy influence the actions of your sales team?

I've made it a kind of informal research project. I have now collected responses from more than a hundred CEOs and more than a thousand sales reps. The executives rate the sales team's understanding of the company strategy at 6.4, and the sales reps put their own understanding at 3.7. The C-suite's perception of how their strategy influenced the actions of the sales team is an average of 5.9, and the sales teams put the level of influence at just 2.7.

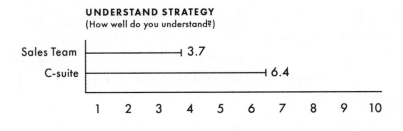

UNDERSTAND STRATEGY
(How well do you understand?)

Sales Team — 3.7

C-suite — 6.4

1 2 3 4 5 6 7 8 9 10

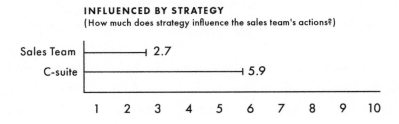

INFLUENCED BY STRATEGY
(How much does strategy influence the sales team's actions?)

Sales Team — 2.7

C-suite — 5.9

1 2 3 4 5 6 7 8 9 10

These are alarming grades. In most high schools, 70 percent is a passing grade. The executives are awarding their sales organization a solid F. But it turns out that the executives are either very generous graders or wildly optimistic. The sellers themselves grade their understanding at 37 percent. Call it an F-minus. The impact of strategy on the actions of the sellers is no better, at just above 50 percent in the executives' estimation and less than 30 percent according to the sellers themselves. This is what failure looks like. Just ask yourself, would you invest in a company with failing grades this dismal? Would you even want to do business with such an organization? Or work for such a company, for that matter?

Among those who did a version of this exercise were the top 100 salespeople of a Fortune 1000 company. It was during their worldwide sales meeting, and at the time, the company was going in a new direction and was relying heavily on its sales organization to make this new direction a success. They would need to sell a broader suite of solutions to a different level of customer in the organization than they were used to working with. These top salespeople understood the new strategy—according to their own estimation—at 28 percent confidence. And this was the top 25 percent of reps in the company! Six months later, their CEO was out the door, and the new direction was completely scrapped with who knows how much money simply written off.

The reason most reps and their managers cannot articulate the company strategy is that C-level leadership does not make enough of a proactive effort to share the strategy. When I ask random employees across functions about the organization's strategy, they typically do not have much to say. I may hear a few widely understood goals, or something that starts to sound a bit like a mission statement, but rarely do I hear any depth of understanding about where the company is heading, how the company is going to win in the market, and their role in the execution of the plan.

No one in the organization will have any depth of understanding of your strategy if they hear it once or twice at annual meetings or town hall updates and occasionally have PowerPoint presentations emailed to them. The components of your strategy need to be woven into discussions at all levels. That includes conversations about how each group and individual is involved in supporting the strategy. It includes conversations about how the work they do contributes to the success or failure of the strategy. These kinds of conversations shouldn't be special events. Rather, they must be a routine part of the way performance is discussed at every level of your business, and the execution of your strategy should be a central part of those conversations.

The sales organization is charged with executing the strategy at the point of the customer. They are literally the front line of customer interaction. To create and maintain a healthy revenue stream, the sales organization needs to have a deep understanding of how the choices they make every day determine the success or failure of the strategy. They need to prioritize the kinds of companies or the level of customer contact they pursue. They choose how they lead meetings with customers, and they surface issues your company can address, emphasize certain products and services, and even prioritize which customer phone calls and emails they address first. Every action they take either reflects your strategy or ignores it, and a huge part of that decision is whether they *understand* that strategy and are clearly made a part of it. If your sales leaders and reps are not sufficiently informed to effectively embody your strategy, you have identified a potential opportunity. If you choose to carry on as usual, your company can continue to chug along, missing out on the power of a sales organization connected to your strategy. But if you choose to empower your sales team to be the front line of your strategy, the benefits are endless.

Sales—and everyone else in your organization—needs a keen-edged message from you and your colleagues in the C-suite. Collis and Rukstad found that, even in the case of the minority of executives in a given company who could give a concise, clear statement of their company's strategy, few of their fellow executives would state it in the same way. The consequences of not having a simple and clear statement of strategy are that the company is "likely to fall into the sorry category of those that have failed to execute" their strategy—or worse, "those that never even had one."[12] They argued that a strategy that addresses their three key components—*objective*, *scope*, and *advantage*—can be stated clearly in a few words.

SALES AT THE CORE OF STRATEGY

As CEO of Tech Data, Bob Dutkowsky led the company to exponential growth. Tech Data grew from $20 to nearly $40 billion and was added to the Fortune 100 under his leadership. He now serves as chairman of the board of US Foods. In an interview with Bob, he described his understanding of how sales must be integrated into the heart of a company's strategy:

> Sales must understand the strategy if it is to execute effectively on every sales call. When sales doesn't embody the strategy—usually because leadership didn't correctly articulate the strategy—the company ends up with a lot of sales, and potentially customers, it really doesn't want. The sales organization is selling at the wrong price, or to the wrong customer, or even selling the wrong products or solutions.

The disconnect between strategy and sales lights up brightly when you need to raise prices or, even more acutely, when you want to launch new products or solutions. Suddenly, you find yourself trying to grow with a sales organization that cannot sell your new offerings at potentially higher prices. While the rest of the organization (R&D, finance, supply chain, etc.) can execute flawlessly to create new competitive solutions, without sales execution, the company and thus the shareholders may never realize the value. Getting the sales organization to understand the strategy and making sure they are prepared to execute it is the job of the CEO and full C-suite.

To execute its transformational strategy, L3Harris CAS is doing just that. They are also putting sales precisely where Frank V. Cespedes, senior lecturer at Harvard Business School, says it should be: at the center of strategy.[13] Positioned here, the sales team creates—it does not merely convey—value. It reveals the solutions that are most meaningful to your specific customer.

Every sales call is an opportunity to actualize the strategy. Those calls are the only place this happens—not in boardrooms, not at the headquarters, not in meeting rooms with internal colleagues. This kind of execution happens only in the field, at the moments when your company meets with customers. It happens before a prospect or client has voted for you with their dollars and made a decision to work with you. The customer's first contact is with sales, the first part of the CX. By placing sales directly in the center of the creation of your strategy and by communicating it clearly and consistently, every day, you help your sales organization do the same with your customers. That is where strategy succeeds or fails.

CHAPTER 2

The Executive's Relationship with Sales

The relationship that the executives and other leaders have with the sales organization is among the most important elements of growth leadership. Very often, that relationship is distant and limited. With more frequency than I'd like to admit, I've seen it as adversarial. And it nearly always lacks a strategic connection. Research on executive involvement with customers and the sales organization fortifies these observations.

Noel Capon and Christoph Senn published a paper in which they concluded that nearly a third of CEOs (28 percent) are deliberately and totally uninvolved with customers or the sales organization. All but 14 percent of top corporate leadership holds itself either completely aloof from customers and sales or is not involved with them on any strategically meaningful level. In other words, nearly nine out of ten CEOs, 86 percent, are completely or significantly disengaged from or misaligned with sales when it comes to determining the direction of their company.[1]

Whether they realize it or not, the third of CEOs who are abdicating their responsibility for customer relationships are making sales responsible for the company strategy. Even among those leaders who do not abdicate totally, the strategic connection between the C-suite and the customer is in varying degrees suboptimal or downright dysfunctional.

You've likely seen this before: A major technology firm had been enjoying success and consistent growth in revenue and net income for years. Then came a patch of flattening growth and shrinking margins. The board brought in a new CEO with a strict mandate to restore growth. Acting on his marching orders, the new CEO invested in several acquisitions intended to broaden the firm's suite of offerings and enable the company to provide end-to-end solutions to customers. The strategy was focused on selling a wider variety of things—technology products and services.

As the acquisitions closed and were folded into the larger company, the pressure on the new CEO became intense. He *had* to show results—beginning now, in this quarter. Accordingly, he decided to motivate the sales team—*hard*.

Every few days, he peppered the leaders of the sales organization with questions about deal progress and calls for forecast updates. They in turn did the same with their direct reports—and they with theirs, all down the line. The conversations were rarely, if ever, about how the company would differentiate and create value in the sales process. Or how the company would provide subject-matter experts to support cross-selling new solutions in early stage opportunities that had great strategic potential. Or how the company would address the organizational challenges to advancing key opportunities. The only substantive conversations with sales were about forecasts. "What are they? Why aren't they higher? They'd better be higher!" The relentless message was unmistakable: "Push harder. The current quarter is all that matters. Everything else can wait."

The CEO took action without a genuinely strategic purpose, and the effect was anything but a tornado of growth. He confounded a tactical *objective* (revenue in the current quarter) with a strategic *goal* (future success sustainable over the long term). Leadership's shortsighted, single-minded message was to just sell now. And sellers will always translate that to mean they should sell what they can to any customer—and not necessarily the most strategic product or customer. The short-term tactic and intensity around it—current revenue is all that matters—eclipsed all the attention that could be directed toward executing the stated growth strategy for the business. The CEO lacked a vision and strategic focus for the sales organization and neither enabled nor required the sales organization to create value by selling in line with a solutions-based strategy. This myopic focus became a toxin that soon cascaded throughout the entire management structure, from the EVP of sales to the sales personnel on the front line, compromising the actions of the sales team every day.

It's commonly understood that more strategic business, the kind of business the CEO of this company wanted, with customers buying broader solutions, doesn't often close as quickly as more transactional product sales. We hear all the time that these sales cycles can be more involved, take longer, and require greater proficiency with a consultative approach. But when pressure to make sales and make them now takes center stage—or, as it did with this company, the entire stage—these realities can get dismissed as excuses. When that happens, the investment in strategy—improving products and services or building new ones, making acquisitions to expand capabilities and offer a wider suite of solutions—falls flat. Further complicating the issue is that it's difficult for sales professionals to toggle back and forth between strategic and transactional approaches to business. It's one or the other.

Month after month, quarter after quarter, sellers focused exclusively on getting whatever deal they could. The faster they could close, the better. Simple sales tactics replaced strategy. Strategic growth gave way to tactical, transactional sales. Sensing the desperation of the sales reps, customers pushed back, holding out for larger and larger discounts, which were invariably approved because of the intense pressure to bring in business, *any* business.

While the sales organization at this tech company was given different things to sell, selling differently—creating a different sales experience—was never a part of the strategy. Since strategy was discarded in pursuit of booking revenue, the result was that the sales organization concentrated neither on selling those different things (in which the company had so heavily invested) nor on selling things differently. As a result, the new solutions and bundled offerings never reached anything close to the projections they'd made.

The typical relationship between the CEO and their sales team is distant at best and antagonistic at worst. Even though many leaders are conversant in the long-standing ideas about sales being more consultative and focused on selling solutions, their interactions with the sales function have little connection to strategy and the importance of the sales team in executing that strategy.

Much like the technology firm's CEO, too many leaders still default to the traditional and more transactional focus of the sales organization: to pitch and close, period. Salespeople just meet with customers, are charismatic, and tell them how good what we offer is, and close. Even when executives say we need to "sell the value," the follow-up conversation reflects their typical focus on how well the reps can explain how good the company is at what it does. Such conversations rarely integrate the idea of creating a valuable sales experience and using that to connect products and services to the business outcomes the customer wishes to achieve. Remember: Every sales call reflects the success of your strategy or its failure, one customer or prospect interaction at a time.

The financial performance of a business is driven by the quality of the interactions between the sales team and the customers. Assessing the impact of a sales force on revenue and profit growth is challenging, because so many factors can influence growth rates. Harvard Business School researchers examined the relationship between relative growth and sales force ranking by *Sales and Marketing Management* across industries, including healthcare, technology, and business services. That relative impact ranged from 20 to 30 percent in some industries and as much as 40 to 50 percent in others.[2] That contributes a massive boost if you are doing it well—or creates a huge anchor if you fail to give it proper strategic attention and focus.

If you allow sales to be separated from your company's strategy, this shortsighted approach means you are allowing the sales team to dictate your strategy. It doesn't matter what you say your strategy is in the boardroom or in leadership team meetings. What actually happens with customers and during sales calls will tell you what your strategy really is. Is your sales team proactively pursuing meetings with prospects and customers that are a match for your ideal profile, the kind who are likely to have the issues and needs that your products and solutions can address? Or are they spending time with whomever they can and being reactive with requests for proposals? Are they interacting with the proper level of buyers who can authorize purchases for the kinds of business you want? Or are they comfortably engaging with contacts who don't really have the authority to say yes? Are they leading conversations about the customers' business outcomes and making connections focused on how your competitive advantages can help them improve those outcomes? Or do they pitch and present whatever they are most familiar with, often neglecting the larger opportunity in favor of a smaller deal now? Without a strong and aligned relationship between senior leadership and the sales organization, it is unlikely your strategy will have the right connection to the customer. As a result, your product, and maybe even your company, will become commodified.

The leadership mindset that cedes strategy to sales is the same mindset that recognizes no strategic role for sales. Even cut loose from strategy, the sales organization can still make sales, but it is unlikely to develop the kind of value-focused relationships that create collaborative, partnering relationships with customers—the relationships that create loyal customers. To differentiate your company in today's market, you must connect with the customer. You must offer them other value for their business.

COMMON SENSE

The C-suite rarely includes sales leaders in its discussion of CX, and this exclusion may seem like common sense. Many sales interactions are with prospects who are not yet customers. "The sales force," apparently, "are charismatic folks who operate separately."[3] Common sense says that sales is its own thing, separate from other business functions. It's all about charisma. It's not part of the purview of leadership, and vice versa. This is because of a "widespread bias that strategic work like finance, supply chain management, and product development is more sophisticated" than sales. This mistake shows a lack of understanding of what is required to provide an outstanding sales experience that becomes an outstanding CX.

To paraphrase Albert Einstein, common sense is the collection of prejudices acquired by maturity. And when it comes to sales, these prejudices have developed over decades. For most people this commonsense collection of prejudices starts to accumulate early in their career. Early on, a number of preconceptions develop concerning sales. These include the idea that selling is all about making a pitch, being personable and likable and probably extroverted, and simply hitting square-on what the rest of the organization—R&D, leadership, finance—has already teed up. The product and the marketing are right there in front of the seller; all the real work has been done already. The salesperson's role is to just swing, follow through, and not muck it up.

Common sense can be a formidable obstacle to overcome, and we need all the help we can get. Sales is afflicted by stigmas and stereotypes that are not simply inaccurate but obsolete in terms of what is required to be successful selling in today's environment. I titled one of my *Harvard Business Review* articles, "Get Over Your Fear of Sales," by confessing my early fear of sales. I explained that, when I graduated from college, I was unsure of my next step into full-time employment. "Many friends suggested sales. I worried that being in sales would not carry the prestige and credibility I so badly wanted as I started my professional career." So, I took a position in human resources (HR) with a Big Six consulting firm. *HR management* sounded so much better to me than *sales rep*. "In truth, though," I wrote, "I was afraid of sales. The perception. The quotas. I hated the idea of having to be pushy."[4]

After all, many people equate selling with the idea that it's about making people buy things they don't want, don't need, and can't afford. But that is a perception that likely emerged from the turn of the twentieth century. In the early 1900s, hucksters and peddlers were among the few sales jobs listed on the US Census. This image still persists when people think about sales. In his book *To Sell Is Human*, Daniel Pink asked several thousand people the first word that came to mind when they hear "sales" or "selling." This word cloud shows their top twenty-two responses. *Pushy*, *yuck*, and *annoying* stand out among the largest. The proverbial used-car salesman springs to mind. But, today, there are more than twenty-eight census codes that reference professional sales specifically, many of which require tremendous expertise. The world has changed.

© 2013 Daniel H. Pink, reprinted with permission.

This seems to be a common reaction. What stops so many companies from creating the kind of modern selling culture that makes for a strong growth-focused culture? I regularly see three things.

The curse of *Glengarry Glen Ross*

Who can forget the scene in the film version of David Mamet's *Glengarry Glen Ross*? Alec Baldwin, sales manager from hell, proclaims, "ABC—always be closing" as commandments one through ten in the salesman's bible. The thing is, particularly in any kind of complex sale, the early stages of the revenue pipeline are when visions are being imagined, budgets are being established, and scope is being determined. The sales team has—and you in the C-suite have—its opportunity to make the greatest *strategic* impact at this early stage. The execution of strategy has its greatest leverage up front.

ABC is elementary and archaic, and yet, I'm stunned by how often I still hear that "we need people who are great closers."

The truth is that, in a more sophisticated selling environment, closing is often anticlimactic and requires less focus. It's a natural extension of the many small advances in the sales process, not a miraculous turning point. Instead, prepare your sales team to create value early, work with other departments and your subject-matter experts on joint call planning and account strategy, and identify issues that customers may be missing or opportunities they haven't considered.

Habit and the persistence of sales stigma

Never underestimate the power of doing things as you always have, even if there is another—better—way. Similarly, never underestimate the persistence of stereotypes, no matter how dysfunctional they are. The perpetuation of the sales stigma is rooted in our common tendency to be guided by any number of unexamined prejudices, the catechism of ABC included.

The *Wall Street Journal* reported in a 2021 article that a primary barrier to filling sales jobs, which are plentiful and high paying, is the stigma of *Mad Men*–style representatives and used-car salesmen that won't seem to go away.[5] What is astonishing to me is that seven years earlier, the *Wall Street Journal* published an article making the same point that said, "There's a huge stereotype that sales isn't really a career—that either anyone can do it or you're born to it," suggesting that the job of selling was anything but highly skilled and strategic and just about personality. It went on to tease the answer in the subtitle: "'Salesman' Baggage Means Well-Paying Tech-Industry Positions Go Begging." Every few years, we're talking about the same issue. To read both articles is to see a needle unmoved in a half-dozen years.[6]

Driven by the stereotype behind the stigma, we often end up looking in the wrong places for sales staff, and so we recruit the wrong people for what should be a sophisticated, highly skilled profession capable of executing the strategy in which the whole company is invested. The most effective remedy for such inadequate recruiting is—rather than lamenting the lack of impressive candidates—to make the job bigger, more ambitious, more demanding, and far more important. Put sales where it should be, fully integrated into the company strategy. Then recruit accordingly. There is a shortage of people eager to go into sales as it is. So reconceive sales as central to your business strategy. Build *that*, and they will come.

Sales is not recognized as central to the strategy of the business

The commonsense C-suite conception about sales does not flow from ignorance but, I believe, in large measure, results from the limited experience most CEOs have with sales. An analysis of Fortune 1000 companies suggests that between 70 and 80 percent of CEOs developed their expertise in operational or finance roles. Indeed, the top three paths to CEO are via finance, operations, and marketing. Some surveys lump together marketing and sales and conclude that 20 to 25 percent of CEOs come from these disciplines. In my experience, if we cleave off sales from marketing, we find that only a single-digit fraction of CEOs come from a sales background.[7]

The sales–marketing conflict

If your sales organization is disconnected from your strategy, it's likely that every function is also disconnected from it to some extent—and from each other. One common and destructive misalignment is the conflict between marketing and sales. Often, the two functions don't even speak the same language. Except for the profanity when they curse each other.

For the purposes of executing your growth strategy, marketing and sales are two sides of the same coin. They're different disciplines, to be sure, but with symbiotic aims. In the universe of the marketplace, marketing should create the gravitational field that attracts the right customers for the value your business offers. The prospects then

continued

gravitate toward the sellers, who guide them through a strategically founded sales experience that creates value for both the customer and the business.

As a Growth Leader, you foster the alignment between sales and marketing to ensure that both functions work together like they are playing on the same team. Executives must establish clear responsibilities for each function, with shared goals and objectives that can't be achieved without each other. Without common ground, there will be continual discord. If you are in meetings and hear that marketing is doing a great job creating leads but sales isn't converting—or vice versa, that sales is doing incredibly well at winning business but marketing is useless—then the misalignment between the two functions and your strategy is at the heart of the problem.

It isn't true to say that a leader must have come from sales or any other department to understand that function. But a CEO's background and deep knowledge base often informs what they prioritize and value and where they focus their attention. So, it's no surprise that the CEO agenda is jammed with operational and financial topics and, by comparison, a paltry focus on sales. Research on how CEOs spend their days indicates strong preferences for time involved with production (operations), finance, and marketing functions.[8] Furthermore, what little time they spend on decisions about sales is focused on forecast and financial data and is often shaded by misunderstandings and the stigma and stereotypes about what will drive sales results.

None of this is to say that executives need to get in the weeds on sales management. But if the sales experience is, in reality, a critical part of the company differentiation and vital to growth, then it deserves greater strategic focus. Absent a strong intentional effort by an executive to understand the nuance and subtlety of the sales organization and how it operates, it's unlikely they will recognize it as central to the strategy.

When I share my articles on LinkedIn, I hear from sales leaders that the CEO and executives don't understand sales and how that negatively impacts their ability to execute on a growth strategy. Until the sales organization is seen as integral to the value you provide your customers—not just the tactical team to make this quarter's numbers—the C-suite will continue to underrate, undervalue, and underuse them.

The stigma and stereotypes about sales are all based on an old model. Of course, there are plenty of examples in the world of business showing us that old models die hard. And plenty of sales teams today behave like their job is mostly to tell customers about all their company can offer. Of course, they are being managed and led to behave that way. These misguided notions prevent you from taking full advantage of a sales organization that differentiates your business in the market and could become a competitive advantage for your business. Those stigma and stereotypes inform dozens of critical decisions CEOs and executives make about the sales function: the kind of people we recruit, how we manage them, how we pay them, how we develop them, and how we communicate with them.

Shift the narrative. Move beyond the stigma and stereotypes that masquerade as common sense. If you can look past the archaic view of sales, your sales team can be a force for growth, creating value for customers and driving the execution of your strategy every day.

THE PROBLEM WITH SALES

When I ask audiences of CEOs whether their sales organization is producing the kind of revenue results they would like to see, the vast majority tell me they are dissatisfied.

When I follow up by asking why, they generally give me answers like these:

- Their sales professionals aren't actively engaged in the right sales activities to produce results.

- The sales team isn't persuasive enough. They are not persuading customers to buy. They are not closers.

- The sellers are not consultative. They don't offer solutions.

- The salespeople aren't driving hard enough or doing whatever it takes to get the job done.

- Sales is wasting time with prospects who are not worth the effort. They are calling on the wrong customers.

- Sales professionals are coin operated. We apparently need to pay more if we want them to sell more.

- Sales uses internal issues—problems with marketing, accounting, or other departments—to excuse their own failure to sell.

- Individual salespeople have blind spots when it comes to certain accounts. They make assumptions that limit growth.

- They lack persistence and are deterred by a single *no*.

These are all reasonable issues, and there is plenty of truth in all the responses. In fact, they articulate well-known, long-established problems in sales. I could have asked—and did ask—the same question about sales and revenue growth to a group of executives a decade ago. The responses were similar. Despite the massive efforts companies have made in the past decade to address these problems, they persist.

But the leaders' attitudes reveal that reliance on common sense. "Our products and solutions are world-class," one said, "and we have one of the strongest R&D groups in the industry. If only our account managers would do a better job of selling our value to customers!"[9] His focus solely on the products and solutions—with no comment about the value in the sales experience—is revealing. Although he said he wanted his team to sell the company's value, what he really meant was he wants them to *tell* the company's value. He wanted his sales team to be a brochure, but that won't lead to strategic sales. Lisa Earle McLeod, the author of *Selling with Noble*

Purpose, says, "Leaders often believe if they can engrave the right words into the hearts and minds of their salespeople, their team will *finally* be able to sell the full value of their solution."[10]

When talking about the struggles with sales, it's almost Pavlovian for the discussion to turn to compensation. It's one of the few areas in sales that executives pay close attention to as a driver of performance. In part, this is because, in B2B companies, compensation typically represents the largest line item in the sales budget. So, while it needs to be effectively managed, I find that it's typically misused or overused as a means of influencing behavior. It's common to think that sales professionals are driven entirely by money and that compensation plan design is the foremost management tool for building high performance. Yes, everyone needs to be paid, and fair compensation, including commissions, bonuses, and the like, is important. But, having interviewed top salespeople in two dozen industries, I can testify to the fact that the best sellers are not exclusively or even primarily motivated by money—at least any more than most company leaders.[11]

McLeod's research, done over a decade with thousands of salespeople and hundreds of sales teams, revealed that salespeople who sell with a greater purpose than making money, who truly want to make a difference in the lives of their customers, outsell salespeople focused on targets and quotas. Further research from Valerie Good, at Grand Valley State University, revealed that salespeople with a sense of higher purpose have more resilience and put forth more effort over time than salespeople focused on financial incentives.[12]

What's more, if you rely mostly on financial incentives to drive behavior—in sales or any other function—you are not leading strategically. You may even be encouraging transactional sales behavior at the cost of developing strategic business, as well as attracting the wrong kind of sellers. Financial rewards can drive attention, can drive focus, and can even drive effort, but money doesn't make people better. It does not develop the skills required for executing strategy and creating value in the sales process.

Another common complaint is that the sales team, according to the C-suite, often misses the mark. As executives typically see it, leadership builds strategies for growth only to have the sales organization squander a lot of time, energy, and money chasing after the wrong customers. It's natural for leadership to blame sales, which is the final link in the chain. Guilt by proximity seems like good common sense.

Not long ago, I met with an executive VP (EVP) of a Fortune 25 company to discuss his growth strategy. The focus of the discussion was an expansion into a new market segment with a line of highly specialized products. We began talking about the revenue forecast. It was one of those conversations that starts out calm and gradually escalates in emotional intensity. Suddenly, the EVP became downright irate.

"You know," he hissed through gritted teeth, "the kind of business our sales team has been pursuing . . . I have absolutely no idea why we're calling on many of these companies!"

"I understand," I said.

"You *understand?*"

"Yes. You're not alone. A lot of executives tell me that their sales organization often targets prospects that just don't fit the profile outlined in their go-to-market strategy. They're chasing the wrong kind of company. Or they're talking to the right kind of company, but they're working with the wrong level of buyer or stuck in procurement, so they won't ever get a decision. Or the target is not the right size and scale, and they have no chance of generating significant business. Or sales is pursuing transactional opportunities that don't feature our new solutions."

"That's it!" he said.

I understood because I see this misalignment all the time, in almost every company I work with. I spent nearly a decade in the sales training business, and what I saw, over and over again, were companies sending their sales teams to programs to be more consultative or more strategic. But at the C-suite level, the vision and strategy for the sales experience remained unchanged. Absent that connection between the executive agenda and the sales experience, good programs devolve into tips and techniques, rather than drivers of real change. Almost invariably, the overall management approach and sales process encouraged transactional behaviors with incentives that rewarded short-term wins, not strategic victories intended to create long-term customers and sustainably grow revenue. When the problem is with sales, it is usually not about sales. It's about leadership.

Each of these failures is part of a larger issue: The sales team has little purpose beyond hitting their numbers. This is because they are evaluated solely on whether they hit those numbers. The actions, abilities, and choices of sellers reflect what they have been hired to do, what they have been trained to do, and what they've been directed to do by the company's leaders. They are compensated based on those numbers. They are told at every fork in the road that their sole purpose is to sell, sell, sell. When asked, nearly all sales professionals say they believe they are doing exactly what their senior leadership has asked them to do—and they're right! We cannot expect some reinvention of the sales organization to address systemic issues with growth. If your company is struggling with revenue growth, don't look within sales. Look for the root cause at the leadership level.

This is true not only of the sales team but of those who staff every function in the company. If you, as a leader, are truly committed to leading growth, you must find a way to make each of your executive inputs intentional. You must ensure that they inform, guide, and inspire your leaders, your managers, and all employees in every function of the organization.

If, instead, sales were part of the wider company strategy, we'd see these issues disappear. The sales team would know exactly who the right customer is and would focus their pursuit only on those customers. They would help customers see issues they hadn't considered or opportunities they hadn't seen and be able to connect your solutions to the things that their customers would value. And that authentic value would mean the customer would see the sales experience as just as important, just as beneficial, as the product or service it was meant to sell. If sales is where strategy goes to die, it is because the management structure of the organization has isolated sales in a silo. C-suite leadership tasks the sales organization with making sales when it should be enabling and enlisting it to implement strategy. It would not be this way if C-level leaders fully engaged the sales organization in implementing the business strategy created in the C-suite.

SALES IS STRATEGY IN ACTION

As you discover the true scope of sales and the true skill set of the sales organization, reassess your sales organization and its role. How can you use your sellers strategically? How can you empower them to put strategy into action? Does it make sense—putting aside your commonsense biases—to create a C-level seat for sales at your leadership table?

Strategy is acquired neither by osmosis nor infection. If you believe the C-suite is the proper venue for the creation of strategy, you are correct. But the sales organization can never convert that strategy into action without understanding it 100 percent. In too many companies, C-suite leaders keep the strategy to themselves. This is not their intent, of course; it's just a lack of good communication. But it makes alignment from the top to the point of customer contact impossible. Using sales strategically begins by reading sales into the strategy.

When you do read sales into the company strategy, avoid the theoretical. This is not an occasion for busy PowerPoints, vague language, and grandiose proclamations. Instead, translate your company strategy into pragmatic actions sales can take. This is not in any way synonymous with dumbing down the strategy. It is working with the sales leadership to formulate the ways in which the organization must and will convert strategy into action.

The effect of these short-term steps is to bring intentionality into the relationship between the C-suite and sales. The small step of making each C-suite input strategic can be leveraged into a large positive impact in the marketplace.

CHAPTER 3

Where Strategy Goes to Die

Whenever I speak at conferences, one of the common refrains I hear from CEOs is that they need their sales force to do a better job of selling to business outcomes, being more consultative, becoming a trusted advisor, and focusing more on offering solutions and less on simply transacting sales. That's right: They see it, and they know it's missing, but their actions don't match their words. The sales force is not selling value because they are not led to do so. The fundamental relationship between the C-suite and sales can play out very differently, depending on how you do or do not foster it.

Long before I started advising CEOs and their teams, I was hired as a sales associate at a company called Learning International, a training and consulting firm that began as the world-famous Xerox Learning Systems and was known for its flagship sales training program, Professional Selling Skills. We were part of a Fortune 500 publishing company. Happily for me, I succeeded in that first-time selling job. Unhappily for Learning International, it failed to meet its strategic goals, at least during my time there. The disconnect between my success and the company's failure was rich with lessons in the persistent disconnect between sales and leadership that exists in most companies today. In fact, these lessons guided me as I advanced to senior VP and EVP roles and finally started my own practice as a management consultant specializing in leading growth.

Back in 1996, the Learning International executive team had an ambitious vision to transform the company's position in the market by rapidly rebranding itself as an "organizational sales performance company." By the time I went to work for the company, that vision had already driven several high-ticket acquisitions in what was then called *technology enabled selling*, or TES. This field was titled with the intention of using technology to provide sellers with the information they need to support the sales process. It quickly evolved into SFA (sales force automation) systems and widened the focus to include automating sales tasks, which then led to CRM (customer relationship management) systems, as they are called today. The new name broadened the mandate further to connect sales with all of the other functions in business to coordinate actions from marketing to supply chain and everything in between—all focused on the customer relationship. Like all technology, CRM has evolved considerably in the last twenty years, but the intent is still much the same: to use technology to help increase sales.

The centerpiece of Learning International's early CRM offering was Heatseeker. It was a fun name built on a compelling metaphor. A heatseeker is an air-to-air missile that homes in on the hot exhaust of a jet engine. Fire a heatseeker in the general direction of the target you want to hit, and it will automatically find the heat and take the missile right to the target. You don't have to make fancy calculations or make as much of an effort to aim. You fire, and the heatseeker makes it easy and does the rest. This system promised to be a machine to make money for our target market of Fortune 1000 companies.

The name was great and the metaphor seductive, but Heatseeker was not simply a product. It was an important part of a transformation. Offering this kind of technology combined with our world-class training programs would give us a much broader range of solutions. On the surface, the Heatseeker acquisition seemed like a no-brainer. It represented a bold evolutionary step. Our company had articulated a compelling vision to become a sales performance company, and now it had acquired a new technology capability that would be key to driving that vision. I was living in San Francisco and selling throughout Silicon Valley at the height of the dot-com boom. What could go wrong?

Unfortunately, vision is not strategy.

Vision is essential, but it is also permanently—and intentionally—aspirational. It is about a long-term future state and encompasses a sense of purpose as well. Strategy has an element of aspiration too, in that the result hasn't happened yet, but the key difference is that strategy is centered on the actions you take to make it happen, on its implementation. Vision is a way to express what you want your company to be; strategy is what your company wants to *do*. That makes vision critically important, to be sure, but for this future to be realized, it must become operationalized. That is the province and function of strategy, which depicts what you are going to do to get there. Strategy is much more about the decisions and choices you'll make and the actions you'll take to fulfill that vision. It must directly drive execution in all functions.

But when it was time to develop a new strategy, Learning International was loose, even hazy. Essentially, their strategy was little more than adding a CRM system to their other products to provide more sales training. It was a superficial improvement. There was little focus on the customer's need or how we would integrate our offerings to create a memorable customer experience. You've likely seen this happen with companies as they launch new products or acquire companies and capabilities to create a larger portfolio of offerings to sell in the market and create more of a one-stop shop or end-to-end solution. You see it when companies move from only selling products to adding a variety of services that pull through products as part of a larger engagement, and as companies shift their business to an SaaS (software as a service) model or now XaaS (anything as a service). A subscription or membership approach may drive longer-term predictable revenue, but only if you connect with a customer in a way that makes them want to sign up—and keep paying.

These methods can, of course, provide more value for customers. But a lack of connection to the sales organization will scuttle the effort. Selling this integrated approach or longer-term service will be substantively different from selling the individual components. How many times have companies excitedly invested in new products or services—new things to offer—only to see disappointing results because the sales organization was not prepared to drive them in the market?

It's a bit like Kevin Costner hearing the voice in *Field of Dreams* say, "If you build it, [they] will come": If you can build the right products, services, and capabilities, the customers will simply come to you, right? But few products and even fewer complex solutions sell themselves. Products and services are not enough to solidify a competitive advantage. If you build it (or acquire it), you must also sell it, and doing so often requires selling differently. That won't happen by declaring that you can now provide much more or much broader or even much better solutions.

I hasten to point out that Learning International was by no means unusual in being long on vision but short on strategy. In that previously mentioned article for *Harvard Business Review*, "Can You Say What Your Strategy Is?," Collis and Rukstad wondered what would happen if you asked top executives two straightforward questions: "Can you summarize your company's strategy . . . [and] If so, would your colleagues put it the same way?" The idea is that most executives struggle to explain their strategy succinctly and clearly. The two authors concluded that "very few executives can honestly answer these simple questions in the affirmative." They refer to this as a "dirty little secret" in business. Few leaders are clear and succinct when they communicate strategy. As a consequence, they are likely to fail to develop a strategy or, if they have one, fail to execute it. In contrast, those very few executives who *can* answer Collis and Rukstad's questions likely "work for . . . the most successful [firms] in their industry."[1] These are clearly Growth Leaders.

CRM systems were new and held great promise, but neither Learning

International nor our customers possessed a deep understanding of Heatseeker. The company had bought, not developed, the technology. Suddenly, instead of just offering development programs to sales organizations—something it had long excelled at—Learning International decided to roll out a broad array of solutions to address virtually everything a sales organization needed. This was not a radically original idea. At the time, our biggest competitor was Siebel Systems, led by Tom Siebel, the author of *Virtual Selling*, which extolled the virtues of technology-enabled selling. They were the market leader in SFA solutions and would ultimately become part of technology giant Oracle. Learning International's vision was to follow Siebel's lead into the rapidly growing market adjacent to Learning International's core business. Unfortunately, the leadership at Learning International failed to articulate a strategy—to themselves, much less to the sales team—beyond the idea that we would have a broad suite of solutions to sell.

As for me, I admit it: I absolutely loved this new direction. I was excited about being in the business of selling technology-enabled *solutions*, not only training products, to blue-chip companies. Fortunately for me, during that first year on the job, I was part of a savvy sales organization with an excellent manager and was assigned a wary and wise mentor in the sales organization. My mentor was a top performer in the company and very skilled. He was thoughtful and cared about the future of the company. Both were exceptional coaches and interested in helping me develop in the profession.

"Cool your jets on Heatseeker," he advised me. "Focus on PSS" (our best-selling sales training program) "and our core training curriculum. It's proven, and our clients love it. All this other stuff is just a distraction, at least for now. Look, no one knows if it even works."

As jazzed as I was by the Heatseeker vision, I did manage to see beyond the reddish haze of my own adrenaline. I recognized solid advice when I heard it. Furthermore, some other top performers in sales were advising much the same thing. I decided that my personal priority in my rookie year was to make my sales quota. And when I blew by the hype and instead examined the current figures, Heatseeker just wasn't selling like it was supposed to, vision or no vision.

Regardless of what the executives said, the actions we took in the field with customers every day were determined by how they evaluated us: win business—any business. That was the company's real strategy, whether the leadership knew it or not. We had the opportunity, based on our actions and decisions, to determine where we spent our time and what we focused on. Absent a strong connection to the company's nominal strategy, we would sell what we were comfortable with and knew best. I ran with PSS. I prospected, developed opportunities, and took meetings to sell that proven product, which meant that about two-thirds of my time was spent with companies that were outside the stated target of Fortune 1000 customers. Even when I did get inside a Fortune 1000 company, my go-to product remained PSS and its supporting programs, rarely the new programs. I sold strategically and consultatively, as I was coached to, digging into the issues they were struggling with and connecting our programs to the business outcomes customers were trying to achieve. But I always went after the deal I knew we could win and implement successfully. In fact, I never sold Heatseeker—not once. The company strategy, from the markets and ideal client profile to the competitive advantage in the market, didn't have much influence over our day-to-day activity, no matter how clear it seemed in the boardroom.

As my own numbers ticked up, I started hearing horror stories from sellers who had made the commitment to Heatseeker that I had not. The sales cycles involved with this system were different from selling training programs. The automation Heatseeker offered made it much more than a *sales* platform; it was an *enterprise* platform, which required a fundamental shift in the sales process and took considerably longer. The issues clients would face in implementation were different, the decision-makers and criteria were different, and our expertise, while exceptional when it came to sales effectiveness, was considerably weaker in the technology arena. That required additional technology resources to support sales cycles, which doubled and tripled the cost of sale. Combined with Heatseeker's complexity, which required customization to fit each client, it was difficult to make the vision for the company a reality.

I soon began hearing my sales colleagues swearing—and I do mean *swearing*—that they would never try selling Heatseeker again. There was simply too little reward for the high risk. The nature of the risk was damaging good client relationships. Everyone was devoting inordinate amounts of time to fighting fires as customer after customer could not even get the system properly installed, let alone up and running.

Heatseeker really had two issues, but they both amounted to a misalignment of the organization's various functions with a single clear strategy. One of the issues was that the product itself required further development and maturation. The company's leadership was not prepared for the ongoing development costs involved in software design, which differed considerably from the costs of designing training programs. But even if the bugs were all magically converted into features, the second problem would remain unresolved: Heatseeker required a fundamentally different sales experience. The sales team needed the ability to help clients address the issues in an enterprise-wide technology implementation. It required a conversation beyond the business outcomes and considerations we were used to discussing. And we weren't prepared for that. When we got to the discussion of technology issues and decisions, we simply didn't have—and weren't given—the tools we needed. No amount of knowledge and expertise in sales performance could make up for this weakness. The Learning International sales force was among the most respected in the training industry and was capable of selling Heatseeker, as evidenced by some early wins. But as an organization, we were not strategically prepared for what it would take to sell this far more varied solution set.

The leadership of the company never fully grasped this. They rarely even interacted with the sales team. The sales organization was certainly never prioritized when it came to communicating the strategy and providing resources to help us execute on these more challenging sales cycles. We understood the vision but had never been read into the strategy required to operationalize it. Our mandate was simply to go forth and sell it. We had built it, so surely the customers should come.

Learning International's sales team was disconnected from the company strategy and had no voice in its formulation or modification. Equally as important, the CEO and the company's executives had become dismissive of the sales team. If sales sent feedback up to top management, such as reporting customer issues with Heatseeker, the leaders upstairs spurned this valuable customer input as just so many sales organization excuses about why they couldn't sell more. The C-suite never saw the challenges we were having as a lack of strategic guidance and the absence of their connection to the market realities. Frustrations and internal finger pointing were escalating. The only guidance we sellers received was to "Go sell everything! We're a sales performance company!"

It was one misfire after another. New products didn't launch, and management struggled to adjust by setting new objectives, frequently with conflicting goals. As the company lost market share, it downsized. Soon, Learning International was no more, absorbed in a merger with other training organizations.

The absence of a vital link between C-suite and sales meant that sales was largely in the dark about strategy. And, in turn, management was in the dark about what was or was not working in the field. This made an effective organizational strategy—that is, one that could be executed—impossible. The C-suite leaders were cut off from sellers and, therefore, from their customers. This meant that what passed as a strategy failed to deliver an executable *what*. It did not specify any of these crucial aspects of the business:

- This is what we are going to do.

- These are our objectives.

- Here is our part of the market.

- Here is how we're going to compete and win in our part of the market.

To supply this missing material, the strategy needed to define the role of the sales organization in the execution of the strategy. This definition is essential to breathing life into an unexecuted strategy. These specifics are the missing link between strategy and execution. The absence of a direct line of sight between leadership and the sales organization is why that link is missing.

Learning International was hardly unique in suffering from that missing link. In fact, it was not the exception but the rule. C-suite sets the strategy and then too often turns a blind eye to how the sales team executes. All leadership demands from its sales organization are sales. Inevitably, then, sales becomes the place where strategy goes to die.

CUSTOMER VALUE AT THE HEART

Inadvertently limiting your sales organization to meeting quarterly quotas is an all-too-common form of self-sabotage. But *common* does not mean *inevitable*. Take Edwards Lifesciences, a publicly traded medical technology company with revenue of more than $5 billion. John Kiriako has been one of the company's top-performing field sales representatives for the past decade. When I spoke with John and his colleagues, I quickly recognized that the company has a productively disruptive approach to revenue growth. In fact, the sales professionals there hardly ever talk about making *a* sale. As John wrote to me:

> A very important part of our mission is to always put patients first. It's not about the sale. It's about doing what is right for the patient on the table. We talk about it all the time, in the group setting and even during one-on-one calls. We think, *What if our mom or dad was on that table?* and we act accordingly.
>
> This mission comes straight from the CEO, and we all live and breathe it. I think our clients recognize that, and it builds trust and credibility. That trust leads to a partnership that builds loyalty—and revenue growth.[2]

Edwards salespeople like to tell you about the time they spend in operating rooms, standing shoulder to shoulder with cardiac surgeons as they perform heart surgeries, directly supporting the implantation of Edwards Lifesciences technologies. Because of their expertise concerning the company's products—heart valves and monitoring devices—these sellers bring high value to the surgeons by helping to guide technically challenging procedures. They also assist both physicians and hospitals in preparing and orchestrating the entire surgical staff for a more efficient surgery that applies tested best practices to the use of Edwards's technologies. These sales reps don't sell different things. They sell things differently. They have become, effectively, copilots to the surgeon.

Among firms that make advanced medical technology, sales representatives often play a consultative role. They must be knowledgeable about the products in question and their applications. Edwards Lifesciences, however, takes this several steps further. Sales reps are critical to the customer experience, and they are instrumental in differentiating their company's value proposition from others'. In the case of Edwards, the sales reps are empowered to enhance the success of the customer. Indeed, the reps bring to every sales call a mission they have in common with the physicians they serve: Both put the patient first. The value of the product is measured in the enhancement of the patient's health and well-being.

The involvement of this medical company's sales reps at the very point of application improves efficiency and effectiveness, reducing the time a patient spends on a heart–lung bypass machine during surgery, which is a critical factor in everything from successful recoveries to reduced infection rates. This efficiency also reduces operating room time and costs, which are important financial metrics for hospitals.

John and his colleagues are no doubt talented and skilled sales professionals, but their success does not happen in the isolation of the sales organization. And that is precisely the point. The CEO of Edwards, Mike Mussallem, regularly acknowledges the importance of what the sales representatives do for patients as a primary relevant differentiator in his business.

The experience and value these reps provide to cardiologists and cardiac surgeons play a critical role in creating patient success. That medical and administrative staffs appreciate this is reflected in their loyalty as consumers of Edwards's products. Revenue growth and financial success have been exceptional at the company. The top line has grown more than 10 percent in each of the last ten years, while the stock price has increased nearly 4,000 percent. The business has grown from just over $2 billion in sales to more than $5 billion in the span of five years.

Investor's Business Daily noted that Edwards invests more than any other med tech company in heart valves and is always fast to the market with innovative products.[3] But CEO Mussallem's comments about integrating the sales experience make it clear that having great products is only one term in the equation of his company's success. He understands the vital role of the sales organization in providing real solutions to Edwards's customers.

In an interview with Mussallem, he told our team that:

> Innovating in healthcare with the bold goal of changing the practice of medicine and patient care is a team effort. Throughout the history of Edwards Lifesciences, the collaboration between physicians or healthcare professionals and our Edwards employees—each bringing their own expertise and perspective to solving patient challenges—has resulted in far better advances than those working alone. Our focus in introducing new medical technologies always begins with achieving procedural success for the patient. In addition, our sales organization and the experience we deliver with relationships developed through partnerships for patient care are a critical part of our success. They will provide insights based on their experience and data on how to approach a case, which therapy to use—even if it is not one from Edwards—and what ultimately will help that patient return to health. We know that when the patient experience is positive and we and our partners do right by the patient, everything else will fall into place, and the company will succeed.

Edwards Lifesciences did not randomly luck into finding a talented sales force capable of partnering with surgeons. The recruitment, development, management, and compensation of sales professionals are strategic considerations. That is, the strategy of the business includes the profile of the sales professionals the company recruits, how sales talent is developed, how the sales force is compensated, and, perhaps most significantly, how the success of sales is managed and led. By ensuring that its sales organization is thoroughly enabled and empowered to sell the company's strategic solutions, Edwards Lifesciences establishes a clear line of sight from the very top of the company down through sales and all the way into the world of its customers. Sales reps are hired, trained, led, and evaluated on the basis of strategy implementation, not just outdated stereotypes.

Resist the temptation to write off the lessons of Edwards Lifesciences as being applicable only to the healthcare industry. True, the path of disruption was perhaps more familiar for a maker of medical technologies than it would be in some other industries, but the principles can be applied to virtually any business. Edwards's sales reps functionally become part of both the company's strategic team and the hospital's surgical team. Sales reps, executives, surgeons, and patients are united in a profitable and productive enterprise. Any organization can and should admire this model and carry away from it all that it can grab.

Like other companies, Edwards Lifesciences has a C-suite leadership responsible for formulating strategy and policy. Unlike most other companies, it ensures that the sales organization is thoroughly prepared to sell the company strategy to customer decision-makers. The sellers forge powerful links between company and customer so that genuine solutions are created for physicians, hospitals, and patients. To be sure, these solutions are sold. Sales *are* made and revenue *is* generated, but each sale is a deep and ongoing relationship and not the result of a one-off transaction or a series of transactions. The resulting revenue, therefore, tends to be sustainable over the long term. Instead of settling for making sales, Edwards aspires to create customers—long-term, high-value customers.

It is the responsibility of leaders in the C-suite to help your leadership teams design and implement processes that facilitate communication and collaboration while also fostering a culture of teamwork between the functions of your organization.[4] Establish a feedback loop between sales and the CEO—and between all other functions. Give the leadership of sales ample opportunity to contribute to and weigh in on strategy and to ensure that sellers deliver customer feedback all the way to the top. Leaven marketing research with feedback and insights from the sellers in the field. Sales is naturally positioned to be a fertile source of ground-level market intelligence, so use it!

OVERCOME YOUR BIAS AND FEAR

Involving sales in strategy is most thoroughly done by giving sales, as a core business function, the right seat at the executive roundtable—so what stops leadership from productively linking sales to strategy? The existence of sales stereotypes as extroverted closers with a fire in the belly is certainly part of it. The stigma around sales doesn't create a sense of strategy execution. This bias is often based on leadership's limited personal experience with sales. The C-suite's assumption is that sales, even when consultative, is not strategic in nature. Remarkably few leaders understand the role and value of the sales organization as a driver of strategy.

But there is also an element of fear. Some leaders are afraid that if they focus their sales organization on strategy implementation, sales may stop hitting their numbers. There is a sense that taking the time to involve sales in strategy is like taking the foot off the gas. When leaders are scared, they frequently want to stomp that pedal by increasing sales activity. More customer calls means more sales, right?

Well, I worked with a provider of IT products and services that began a major push of sales activity. Their orders increased by more than 11 percent, but their total revenue declined by 6 percent. As their sellers chased any business they could close, the average account potential shrank, and order size declined.[5]

The truth is that leadership's overzealous and shortsighted pressure on sales professionals is uniquely counterproductive. It simultaneously drives sales behavior that usually fails with customers and encourages the pursuit of bad business just to make a number. Those kinds of numbers are frequently suboptimal. Getting more strategic with the sales organization doesn't mean taking an eye off the ball of current opportunities that are worthwhile and likely to produce. Quite the opposite. Just look at Edwards Lifesciences. If your sales calls are, in themselves, valuable to your customer, you will gain— not lose—revenue.

In the short term, you likely benefit from refocusing the time and energy spent pursuing the wrong kind of business that rarely closed to instead focus on more productive pursuit of the right opportunities. In fact, you may find that, in the long term, you have a far greater chance to influence those quarterly numbers so that they both increase at an acceptable rate and reflect the kind of recurring revenue stream you desire.

If you see any drop at all, it is unlikely to be significant or material in the bigger picture. What's more, every company has business they should let go of to effectively grow. But that is a choice you as a Growth Leader get to make. You get to decide how you approach these decisions. The key is that deciding who to pursue and keep as clients, as well as who to dismiss or manage differently, must be part of your strategy. It must be intentionally and systematically implemented.

LEADING SALES TO STRATEGY

Learning International's sales force was an excellent sales force in its market of employee training. The company's new strategy was to broaden its offerings to include the sales process and CRM market and to include all areas of sales performance. But the leadership assumed a talented sales team could just go sell additional stuff to make that happen. Sales wasn't connected to the strategy, and the new product required a very different kind of sale. This is precisely what so many companies face when they launch new products, expand with new services, approach new markets, and aim to reinvent themselves.

In contrast, instead of surrendering to chaos by failing to strategically calibrate the relationship between leadership inputs (strategic decisions) and sales outputs, the Edwards management team ensured that their strategic inputs drove predictable, positive results in sales, profits, and relationships. The top leadership communicates strategic goals in clear and intentional ways, and everyone shares the same vision and the same understanding of the company's objectives. The sellers create veritable partnerships with the company's customers and even stand next to the surgeon in the operating room, eager to coach that physician in how best to use the company's advanced medical technologies. At Edwards Lifesciences, the line of sight is always unobstructed.

CHAPTER 4

The Five Flag Start

Throughout history, flags have been used to communicate. They communicate boundaries, rules, directions, targets, and so forth. When everyone playing and watching understands what they are for, the flags—like any other form of communication—create a shared understanding. Think of the flags used today in the sport of auto racing. They are clear, emphatic communication devices about action and direction. Whether it's Le Mans or the Indy 500, an auto race is all about moving toward a desired strategic result—namely, victory as defined by being the first to cross the finish line at the end of the race. Of course, before you can achieve any result, you must start. The start of an auto race is usually signaled by a green flag. You don't have to be a professional racer to know that green means *go*.

The start flag, which consists of nothing more than a solid green piece of cloth, doesn't get any simpler, and its message couldn't be more straightforward or less ambiguous. In the context of an organized auto race, such as a NASCAR race, the message of the flag is more than simply *go*. It is a signal that the track is ready for the contest, which means that everything along the track has been prepared, inspected, and made safe. The action the flag instigates is simple—*go*—but the context that is also communicated by this flag gives drivers the confidence that the course ahead of them is ready and, at least for now, free from hazards.

The wave of that green flag is a trigger, an instruction, a permission, an assurance, and, not least, an inspiration. It starts the adrenaline flowing in racers and fans alike, and it communicates as much information and certainty as it is possible to make available at the starting time. Simple as it is, then, the message of the green flag is also surprisingly rich with useful information.

Moreover, the action that it instigates gives strategic meaning to that action. It starts all the cars at the same time. Not a single car can start to race until the green flag is waved. This transforms what would otherwise be nothing more than the movement of a collection of cars into a *race*, a movement of cars with a strategic purpose defined by a desired result, which is measured precisely, objectively, and in a way that is meaningful to every stakeholder—drivers, owners, spectators, sportswriters, gamblers, you name it.

In business, there is a similarly simple and direct yet richly meaningful set of communications to signal leaders at every level in a business that their strategy is ready to be executed—or not yet ready, as the case may be. This signal should get everybody started, together, headed in the same direction, moving toward the same strategic goals and at the right time. But guiding the creation, launch, and execution of a business strategy is more complex than starting an auto race. A single flag won't do the job, so I've divided the message into five. These five flags each signal that one aspect of a growth-focused strategy is both executable and ready for execution. To get the race moving, you need a Five Flag Start.

THE FIVE FLAG START

George Box, a British statistician, said, "All models are wrong, but some are useful."[1] His point was that, even if a model didn't perfectly represent reality—because none can—it may offer insight or practical actions that improve your situation. The first three flags in my Five Flag Start will be familiar and common elements of most strategy models. My emphasis here is on the clarity and precision that makes these flags useful for execution in the field.

Flag 4 makes the sales experience central to strategy; this is likely new to you outside this book. Flag 5 creates the bridge from strategy to execution. The last two flags are rare in any strategy model, and my inclusion and synthesis of these five flags is what makes the model unique and, more importantly, useful.

FLAG 1: WHAT DEFINES SUCCESS?

Years ago, on a Hawaiian vacation, I saw a T-shirt in a souvenir shop window. Emblazoned across the chest was the quotation "The unaimed arrow never misses."[2] Although I didn't buy the shirt, I've remembered it for a long time because I saw something beautiful in its essence. Letting your arrow fly without a set target—staying loose and open to the possibilities of serendipity—can lead a person to great experiences, unforeseen inspiration, and maybe even enlightenment. But while the unaimed arrow approach holds some promise for living your life, it's just plain bad for business.

The first signal of our Five Flag Start is to define success. This is central to our framework because it is central to your business. If you and your employees don't know what it means to be successful, you have no way to guarantee you'll get there—or even that you're driving in the same direction. Success is the ultimate results of your strategy, the highest-level goals. What does that look like for your company? If what your team does brings that objective closer, they are succeeding. Your definition of success must be clear, unambiguous, and emphatic. Its message must be universally understood within the organization. It needs to convey the first element in so many familiar strategy models: a compelling objective.

A business needs targets, and the self-evident truth is that your enterprise cannot succeed in reaching a goal that does not exist. Unless the leaders in the C-suite define success before they build a strategy, the company is aimless in the most literal possible sense. Defining success for a particular business in a particular set of circumstances and within a given time frame is, admittedly, more complicated than defining success in archery, but the definition must be made, nevertheless. Success cannot be left as a vague notion. In business, it needs to be quantified and visualized. This makes it a destination as distinct as any bull's-eye.

In leading a business of nearly any kind, success usually has a financial dimension front and center. While it is certainly not the only measure of success, it will always be a major factor within any commercial enterprise. People have many motives for being in business, but none is more universal than making a living. Money is measured in profit and loss, revenue and margin, ROI, competitive ranking, and other such pecuniary categories. All of these make for laser-sharp and objective metrics, which are a great help when you want to paint a neon yellow bull's-eye on your targets.

Within the general definition of success, there are several levels of detail. You must have a long-term vision for what your company will be. But you must also know—and your entire organization must know—how you will get there. To live up to its name, your definition of success must be both visionary and strategic.

Multiple objectives often combine to create a vivid picture of what success looks like, each playing an important role on its own. It almost always includes a financial measure or two, such as revenue and net income. But is a financial measure enough on its own? Rarely. Most of the time, we need more—especially when the strategy involves significant change or growth for an organization. When people in organizations are energized about the work they do, it isn't often about numbers in isolation.

I worked with a company called Vology that sold refurbished IT equipment. They were looking to transform to a full-service IT managed services business. It was not enough just to grow; they needed a particular kind of growth. Their primary objective was to achieve 50 percent of revenue from services over three years (they were starting at less than 10 percent). Of course, revenue and profit were important objectives, but the shift in their mix and type of revenue reflected a significant change in their business that allowed them to achieve a top 25 worldwide ranking on the MSP 501, the information technology channel's comprehensive ranking of managed IT services providers.

A credit union I worked with, GTE Financial, was one of the largest locally owned and operated financial institutions in the nation. It now has more than 200,000 members.[3] In addition to some financial metrics, the critical performance indicator that, to their leadership, would drive everything was to improve the member experience. The firm had emerged from some major struggles with a Net Promoter Score in the negatives.[4] Getting that score into the 60s or 70s would mark a considerable achievement and would represent a shift in focus to the member experience.

Another client, Exact Sciences, best known for Cologuard, its noninvasive at-home colon cancer screening product, connects its financial success to changing lives. The number of tests they administer each year is one of the company's key drivers of financial performance. (Cologuard currently generates more than $1B annually.) Beyond the financial impact, each test provides an opportunity for the early detection and treatment of colon cancer. Like many other kinds of cancer, colon cancer is far more treatable when detected in its early stages. Jake Orville, general manager of the Screening Business, which includes Cologuard and a variety of other screening tests, says that "connecting the tests we complete to the early detection of colon cancer can have a significant impact on patient outcomes. It's part of how we sustain our energy and focus on the work we have to do."

You're looking for a combination of objectives that say, "This is what would make our company successful in 1–3 years." Your objective is to establish a positive and intentional change that you can rally your organization behind. Financial measures are valuable, and most sets of objectives are incomplete without them. But painting a fuller picture of what meaningful success really looks like is vitally important for the Growth Leader.

The first flag forces you to understand and communicate the objective of your strategy. Renowned strategy authors Michael Porter, A. G. Lafley and Roger Martin, and David J. Collis and Michael G. Rukstad have all written in terms of objectives and goals. This is the crucial first step to getting where you want to go: knowing *where* that is.

FLAG 2: WHAT IS YOUR POWER PLAY?

The second flag is about your product, service, or capabilities. It calls for a definition of your differentiation in its most direct sense: What do you have, what can you offer, and what can you do that others do not have, cannot offer, and cannot do? Or, at a minimum, what can you do better than others? What is your power play—your unfair competitive advantage? I call that advantage your power play, based on the hockey term I've come to appreciate. (As a Floridian, I did not grow up around hockey, and I get that hockey is not top of mind when people think of Florida. But the Tampa Bay Lightning—the team we locals call the Bolts—won Stanley Cups in 2004, 2020, and 2021, and they've only been around since 1992.) Now, if you are a hockey fan, you know that *power play* has a specific definition in the game. A hockey team is said to be on a power play when at least one opposing player is idled in the penalty box, giving your team a numerical advantage on the ice.

What's important about this is that a numerical advantage is a fact, not a claim and not an opinion. In your business, your power play must also be a fact-based advantage. It must be real and objectively or at least observably definable. For you as a CEO, the question that defines the power play is this: *Why are consumers going to choose us in the face of competing alternatives that look similar or even the same?* This isn't a laundry list of every feature or benefit your company possesses. It's an honest assessment of the reasons why customers choose you. For most companies, there are two or three reasons that make the difference for them in the eyes of customers.

Peet's Coffee found their power plays and learned how to use them. The company was launched on April 1, 1966, when Alfred Peet opened a coffee store in Berkeley, California. He had grown up working in his father's coffee roasting and grinding business in the Netherlands. He worked in the tea business in Indonesia in the 1950s and was introduced to darkly roasted coffee beans while there. He came to the United States and saw a need for dark roast. As he put it, "I came to the richest country in the world, so why are they drinking the lousiest coffee?"[5] He started a coffee-importing business in California, and his dark-roasted beans were a market differentiator—his power play—since virtually nobody else at the time was marketing dark-roast coffee to American consumers.

The dark-roast coffees became the primary feature of his coffee shop at Vine and Walnut, in Berkeley, near the university campus. Within a year of opening his store, however, Peet began to promote another power play: the freshness of his coffee. Not only was it freshly ground, but the beans themselves were super fresh.

In the 1970s, Peet's began expanding and today has more than two hundred retail locations. The company also sells its coffee in some 14,000 grocery stores and online. Eric Lauterbach, the current president of Peet's, came to the company to lead the consumer division. Since his arrival at the company, they have tripled their revenue, in part by focusing more sharply on freshness as the company's power play. Peet's had developed a direct grocery store delivery system that ensured a continuous cycle of fresh beans on the shelves and rotation of stock to ensure it. None of the other major specialty coffee companies, including Starbucks, had that delivery system or enacted stock rotation that would allow them to rival Peet's approach. This makes Peet's freshness both a genuine advantage and a differentiating feature since no one else offers it.

In fact, competitors have a strong disincentive when it comes to freshness. The only way to ensure freshness is to ensure delivery of super-fresh beans. Most coffees arrive in stores through the same wholesale distribution channels, of which the giant Sysco is the best known. Such distributors are the industry standard, and it works well enough for a shelf-stable product like coffee, which doesn't spoil in the way that milk turns sour or leafy green vegetables turn leafy brown. What Peet's management understood is that just because the beans don't outright spoil, it does not mean that old beans are as good as fresh beans.

In terms of flavor, coffee beans are best right out of the roaster. "Caramelization is at the perfect point of development, and the oils are at their most complex and aromatic . . . Over time, that complexity is lost. Aging is a subtractive process. The oils go dull and flat, and the more delicate aromas dissipate. The beans' signature flavors lose their luster."[6] The only way to ensure this level of flavor-preserving freshness is to shorten the time between roasting and delivery to stores. Peet's understood that this required investing in a proprietary, dedicated delivery system, which is much faster than what the common-carrier wholesalers can deliver.

Direct delivery is, of course, a significantly more costly method of fulfillment. Unless your differentiation depends on freshness, creating your own direct delivery system is like reinventing the wheel, an unnecessary expense. If, however, you see in freshness your power play—your competitive advantage—it is an absolutely necessary investment.

Eric himself will tell you, as he has told me, that freshness certainly comes at a price premium. So, this power play dictates that Peet's focus its market not just on the specialty coffee sector but on that slice of that sector consisting of consumers who put a high value on freshness. While this slice is a subset of a subset, it is made up of loyal strategic customers who are willing to buy the super-fresh product in which Peet's has invested a dedicated delivery system.

Peet's power play is found in the taste profile and freshness of its coffee, which Peet's customers are willing to pay more for. Companies that successfully leverage their power play offer something—some combination of value—that others do not have but that some sufficient segment of the market wants to buy.

All's unfair

You'll notice from the story that Peet's didn't rely on only one power play throughout the life of the company. They found a power play—dark roast—and used it. Their company prospered. But when they found another power play—freshness—that could outclass their opponents, they embraced it. Like in sports, the power play changes on the ice. If a strategy isn't working or another would work better, you need to adapt. Growing in size and brand reputation enables Peet's to compete more effectively on those two differentiators as well, further enhancing their competitive strengths.

A successful strategy leverages the available strengths of the organization, reaping what the company's investments (in personnel, R&D, and so on) have sown. The power play, however, is a special case. It is a strength so clear and so absolute that it almost seems to be an unfair advantage, like playing (however temporarily) with a numerically superior team. In fact, the more absolute or unfair your power play feels, the more powerful it is. Back in the late nineteenth century, John D. Rockefeller saw his power play in vertical integration. His Standard Oil Company started out as an oil-refining business, but Rockefeller soon added to it in the form of pipelines, railroad tank cars, petroleum terminals, and even his own factories to manufacture barrels. Vertical integration (and a host of other even more aggressive moves) gave him a terrific power play, which the federal government eventually decided didn't just *seem* like an unfair advantage but actually *was*.

You don't have to be a John D. Rockefeller to leverage an effective power play. Ultimately, for any company, the power play is all about why customers will choose you and your product over others. The power play is the most relevant differentiator of your value. As the top leadership, therefore, you must know your company's strengths and identify which among them have the greatest potential for differentiation. This subset of strengths makes up your company's available power plays. The objective is to invest strategically to develop them and then play to them.

FLAG 3: WHO WILL VALUE YOUR POWER PLAY?

Your power play is powerless if your customers do not value it. Peet's Coffee invested heavily in a direct delivery system that ensures their coffee beans are always the freshest in the store. The system comes at a cost, and the premium is reflected in the retail price of the coffee. Consumers who want nothing more than a cup to be the delivery system for enough caffeine to bring them out of their morning coma are not likely, given the choice, to pay the price. Peet's does not target these consumers. Instead, the company focuses on those customers who value the fresh flavor of its power play. Besides, it is folly to try to be everything to everyone, especially when you can be everything to those who relish what is special about your product.

The third part of the Five Flag Start calls for you to define who will value your unique power play: your target customer, your ideal customer profile. *Who will value what you have to offer?* You may have read terms such as *scope*, *target market*, or *ideal client profile* in other discussions of this flag. The second and third flags serve to remind us that strategy is about what *not* to do as well as what *to* do. Taken together and aligned, these two flags monetize your competitive advantage.

Know your customer! YOU! The CEO!

If just half of your revenues come from your target market or industry sector, you have identified a potential signal that your strategy isn't getting translated into action. Your sales force is likely spending a great deal of time and effort making sales to customers that are not prioritized in your strategy and thus do not reflect the level of investment you have made with the intention of selling to those specific markets or industries. If sales is not creating value by making the *right* sales, they are wasting effort and tossing strategy to the wind.

Developing a full understanding of the health of your company's revenue stream is crucial to strategy and its execution. The revenue stream is complex and dynamic and is at the heart of growth. Influencing healthy growth requires strategic intervention at precisely the right points along that stream. But it does not require a detailed knowledge of the revenue stream to understand that 100 percent of that revenue comes from a single source: your customers. This simple fact is the ground truth of your business, and what that tells you is that you—specifically, *you*, the CEO—need to build a great customer experience.

Back at Peet's, Eric Lauterbach understood this when he felt insufficiently enlightened by the marketing team's analytics when business at their iconic Berkeley campus store began to flatten. For all those numbers and spreadsheets, none of the marketing team had actually spoken to a single customer. Having started out in sales at Procter & Gamble, Eric did what he knew worked best when trying to understand customers. He hit the ground, walked into the store, observed, and started some friendly but probing conversations. He learned quickly that it was the company's newer light roast, rather than the dark roast the brand was—and is—best known for, that people were drinking. He asked the store manager about this and was told that light roast was what the younger consumers on campus wanted. In fact, most of the younger crowd did not like the dark roast. He then took this information back to headquarters, and the company began working on a go-to-market strategy that would take into account different age profiles.

Michael Loparco, as the EVP and CEO of Electronics Manufacturing Services (EMS) at Jabil, was no stranger to the front lines either. He would routinely meet with customers and develop intimate relationships, but he also took the bold step of bringing the sales experience directly into the C-suite. He elevated the role of chief sales officer (CSO) for his company as a direct report. His approach was that seating a top sales leader—whose daily mandate was speaking with customers—at the executive roundtable brought the customer experience squarely into a strategic context that made execution more timely, detailed, and effective. This requires much more than simply changing the title of the VP of sales to CSO. It's a fundamentally different way of thinking about the role and how the C-suite maintains an accurate pulse on customer reality.

Whether the top leader ventures out of the office to pay a visit to the customer, brings the customer into the C-suite, or does some of both, what Pinterest cofounder and CEO Ben Silbermann shared at an open forum attended by my researchers is key: "Know your customer!" he said. Then, raising his voice, added, "YOU! The CEO!"

This imperative should come across as a blinding glimpse of the obvious. That's how Silbermann himself takes it. For him, *know your customer* is so important that he regularly sets up listening tours throughout the United States and much of the rest of the world to hear directly from his end users about what Pinterest needs to be doing or doing differently to meet their needs. Such a commitment of time and effort from a busy executive is eloquent testimony to how highly he values such contact.

Lauterbach, Loparco, and Silbermann each preach and practice their own version of the imperative to know your customer. Each injects himself into the customer experience by reaching out to *their* customer, who, by the way, is always a moving target in today's dynamic marketplaces. You can add to these three voices those of Fortune 500 CEOs Bob Dutkowsky and Bill Amelio.

Dutkowsky shared with me and my researchers the nature of his connection to the customer and how he was always determined to understand what the sales organization was living on a day-to-day basis. He does this quite casually and says that it "doesn't matter what the issue is; the importance is high touch. Randomly pick a customer on your list and call." He makes a couple of calls each week to customers, asking them, "How are we helping you? What else can we do?" He listens, asks questions, then listens some more, surrendering the agenda of the phone call to the customer. He explained that, in his company, doing so has a profound impact on strategy.

Bill Amelio relies on his sales organization for customer insight, telling us, "Sales are my CIA. They understand the changing nature of the market. Leadership benefits by listening to that." He went on to say that the intel from sales "determines our strategy," and he described this information as "a gift," even when he was being told something he did not like to hear. My observation is that too many executives would rather regift the negative feedback they receive from prospects and customers and look for blame, rather than take an honest look at where their companies are failing.

In most organizations, growth is more than making your numbers. It calls for acquiring customers who fit within your target market or ideal client profile—that is, customers who buy the solutions in which you have invested heavily and want to sell at optimal margins.

To find that customer and to determine whether the ones you have are the ones you need, you must get to know them. The CEO and C-suite cabinet are usually ensconced in company headquarters. Invariably missing from that HQ are customers. Customers are in the marketplace, out in the world, not in the building. This means that executives rarely have a meaningful conversation with them unless it is proactive and intentional. Without such close contact, you have no way to fit them into your strategy.

Align your power play with your customer

When I started working with another of my clients, PURE Insurance, they were a $250 million company. Today, revenues are over $2 billion and have grown by more than 15 percent annually for fifteen consecutive years. Fast growth can bring risks for any company, and that's especially true in the insurance industry. PURE's growth has been driven by an extraordinary competitive advantage avidly sought by high–net worth individuals yet rarely offered by companies in the largely commodified mainstream homeowner's insurance market. "Insuring high net worth individuals is all we do," PURE's website unabashedly announces. "By focusing entirely on this space—and welcoming only highly responsible members—PURE can offer more generous coverage and fair pricing."

PURE stands for Privilege Underwriters Reciprocal Exchange. The company is a reciprocal insurer whose policyholders are known as members, and the business is designed with a strong sense of mutuality that allows the membership to share in good results. PURE is managed by a separate, for-profit management company called PURE Risk Management. The policyholder-owners effectively spread the risk among themselves. PURE Insurance is by no means the cheapest, but premiums are customized, based on each member's risk factors. Integral to the business model is a highly selective approach to accepting members. For PURE, the strategic customer is one who has unique assets that require care and expertise but also a high sense of responsibility to reduce the chance of ever using the insurance. To further decrease the likelihood of claims, the company offers highly proactive consultation on strategies for risk minimization and loss prevention.

As Ross Buchmueller, CEO of PURE, shared with me, "Finding the right member is paramount to our success. In the insurance industry, growth at any cost is not a good thing. The fact is that anyone can write insurance business in, say, hurricane country like Florida and come away with tremendous top-line growth. Especially in places with higher risks, we need to be extra careful when selecting thoughtful and careful people for membership. We enjoy welcoming new members, but we have to be just as diligent at walking away from opportunities. The objective is not just growth but *strategic* growth. That means finding the right member in the right place and the right time on the right terms. This focus on the right kind of customer for us is vital and balances sales against capital preservation. Our executive team must have a direct line to the sales organization so that the sales team is clear about the kind of members that will drive growth and those potential members that could put our business at unnecessary risk."

Ross went on to explain that PURE's power play begins with the very structure of the company. "Our members are at the center of the company," he says, "and we are all about serving our membership. There's an alignment of interests and goals between us and our members. If we serve them well, we will grow our revenues. If we underwrite and prevent losses, we can keep premiums fair for the membership. It's not perfect, but we are constantly seeking an equilibrium that allows mutual benefits for all stakeholders."

Buying conventional insurance is considered a contingent action. If you suffer a loss, the insurance company comes in and compensates you for that loss. But that doesn't prevent the losses from happening. PURE invests an awful lot of time and energy in preventive action with proactive programs to help its members understand their risks, mitigate them, or eliminate them. The company has a team of risk managers who work directly with members to evaluate risks in their homes and mitigate those risks and help them actually get the work done.

Buchmueller noted in a *New York Times* interview that advising clients does pose certain challenges. "If I say, 'Before you go away, you should turn the water off in your house,' there are only so many people who are going to do that. You feel good about [giving the advice], but you didn't change behavior."[7] So, PURE goes beyond mere advice. It assists. It facilitates. Ross highlights that a common risk with older homes in earthquake-prone California (for instance) is that a quake may sever a gas line, causing a potentially catastrophic leak. Homeowners can install seismic shut-off valves, which will automatically shut off natural gas flow in the event of an earthquake. The devices are not expensive, but they can be a hassle to install. Ross says that a member of the PURE team will make the necessary appointment with a plumber, show up with the necessary parts and tools, and stay until the job is completed. His team understands that their customers are successful people and very busy and, more than anything, just need some help getting the job done. He shared with me that "we can empathize with the busy, successful people we serve and realize that sometimes they need us to get things done, not just offer a few tips."

As Ross shared with me, "We actively work with our members to prevent or minimize loss. For us, this is a big part of strategic selling, and it begins by assuming that customers are ultimately rational. There are no uncooperative insurance customers, just loss prevention reps with bad ideas. If I go to a prospect and say, 'I can make you safer and prevent loss in a cost-effective way,' that person will never tell me, 'No thanks. I like to take risks.' They simply disagree with our recommendations, and we need to improve our ideas, or our communication needs to be more effective."

PURE is not cheap insurance, but it is (the company suggests) fairly priced insurance, given the level of consultative concierge service that min-imizes risk. Besides, the company understands that, for its customers, the issue is not strictly money. "A six-figure check to cover the loss of a beloved piece of art is cold comfort when the wall is bare."[8] It's much better to invest in preventing the loss than in being compensated for it. If this isn't sufficient to win the customer, PURE, as a policyholder-owned company, allocates a portion of any surplus balance (premium revenue versus claims and expenses paid) to subscriber savings accounts.

Clearly, by its highly specific definition of the customer that will value its power play, PURE is radically differentiated from the mass of insurance providers. Its universe of prospective customers is limited, but those cus-tomers are profitable and loyal. The company has renewal rates and Net Promoter Scores that soar above the insurance industry average.[9]

The company extends the strategic approach to customer acquisition to the way it builds its broker network. It does not broadly canvass, invite, or recruit prospective brokers; it appoints them after it is clear there is a good fit in terms of market and values. After all, if you are going to be rigorous about the kind of customers you want to have, then you need to apply the same rigor when establishing your standards for a distribution channel. Ross notes that there are some 25,000 to 30,000 independent insurance brokers and agents in the US. But, as he said to me, "We're very selective with who we work with. First, we must screen out those independent firms if there is any doubt that we can build a higher level of trust. We expect them to be fiercely independent and advocating for their clients, but doing so with integrity. Second, we prefer experts. The advice and quality of the engagement with an insurance broker is paramount to an insurance buying decision. This broker needs to understand and work with us to help assess risk, to deliver a great service proposition to the member without sacrificing their independence." The company currently works with a network of about 1,200 different broker firms. In working with high–net worth clients, the broker has to be a counselor and add value to the transaction. PURE's broker network is a vital part of the connection to its members, and each broker needs to be a consultative customer advocate. The sales experience is strategic in that it adds critical, differentiating value.

Companies like PURE Insurance are not boutique shops but major businesses that meticulously align their power play with customers who value it and are both able and willing to pay for it. This creates differentiation and loyal customers, which makes for a compelling and sustainable competitive advantage.

The strategic customer

The third flag calls for you to identify the kind of consumer who will value the millions—and in plenty of cases, billions—of dollars you have invested in your power play and is willing to pay a premium for it. This is the right customer, who fits your ideal profile and represents an opportunity to move beyond merely making a sale to creating a sustainable relationship. Depending on what your company offers in the market, there may be a range of strategic customer types or a handful of discrete categories of customers that are an excellent strategic fit for you. But it certainly won't be everyone. The third flag requires the discipline to know what kind of customers to walk away from or, at least, to not heavily invest in. This is probably the most violated component of strategy.

Now, I'm not saying that every last penny of your revenue has to come from the ideal customer—far from it. You should absolutely be opportunistic about business when there are easy wins to be racked up. Even if the customer isn't in your ideal profile or buying your most valued solutions, if the business is easy to acquire and easy for you to implement, take as much business as comes your way.

But those two criteria are very important if that business is to be truly opportunistic: It must be both easy to acquire and easy to implement. Companies get into trouble when one of these two criteria is missing.

When the first criterion is missing, the sales cycle is long and difficult, taking up time and resources. It also comes with challenging negotiations that create margin pressure. The time, effort, energy, and money spent on the sale are terribly counterproductive, because they not only go toward the wrong kind of client, but you miss out on allocating those resources toward the pursuit of the right kind of business.

When the second criterion is missing, clients require extra attention, special exceptions, or customization. They may have challenging requirements to fulfill. Again, all of this requires resources for you to deliver for customers that don't have great potential.

Part of Michael Loparco's decision to include sales in the C-suite at Jabil was to ensure the pursuit of the right quality of customer and make the entire customer acquisition process visible as a top priority. Because of the up-front investments required in electronics manufacturing at scale, engaging with a customer who might not represent significant potential for volume and growth could be a costly mistake and, more importantly, a wasted opportunity of limited resources in the ultra-competitive, low-margin EMS world.

So, when opportunities arise that are relatively easy to both acquire and implement, it's great. However, you also have a problem when a large amount of the business your company pursues is opportunistic. Then you have to ask yourself whether your strategy even exists beyond the vague desire for growth.

In the blind pursuit of hitting a quarterly number by selling anything to anybody at any time, you risk squandering the precious resources needed to proactively pursue and acquire the right kind of business that will allow your company to execute its strategy. For Peet's Coffee, a consumer who has no interest in paying more to get the taste of extreme freshness is simply the wrong customer. And because they are clear on that, Peet's doesn't waste time and resources pursuing that segment of the market. They know that in the universe of coffee consumers, there are enough of the right kind of customers for them to succeed. It's critical to know who your right customer is. With that focus, you can go all-in on your efforts to attract them.

FLAG 4: HOW DOES OUR SALES EXPERIENCE CREATE VALUE?

The fourth flag requires you to establish a sales experience that creates value for your customers. If the power play in flag 2 is about the value in what you offer, flag 4 is about the value in how you offer it. Flags 2 and 4 specify the value in what you provide and how you provide it. Plenty of organizations I work with choose to include CX (the customer experience) here as well. That works as long as you are clear that the sales experience is a critical part of the customer experience. As I mentioned in chapter 1, the sales experience is too frequently left out of consideration, which is why it's a prominent component of the fourth flag here.

If part of the purpose of a strategy is to differentiate your brand in the eyes of customers, then the fourth flag is the banner of a core strategic element. By providing value that goes beyond your product, you create loyalty beyond the transaction. You develop important relationships that are drivers for long-term success. When your sales force is fully aligned with your go-to-market strategy, they, as well as anyone in your customer-contact team, will be a significant differentiator of your company. They will add the value that will win the customer's vote—their dollars—for you.

"If only our account managers would do a better job of selling our value to customers!" the hands-off CEO complains. But, having intentionally abdicated leadership of strategy to sales, this CEO misses a fuller or more complete understanding of "our value." In a full strategic view, it won't inhere exclusively in products and services. Rather, value must be based as much on customer relationships as it is on products and services. After all, it accounts for a quarter or more of the decision to do business with you. Approaching value in the customer relationship this way makes it scalable and, therefore, capable of more sustainably differentiating the company's offerings and brand from those of its competitors.

This becomes crucial as companies offer more and more products and services or as they increase in sophistication or when customers are faced with complex choices to determine what they even need to buy. When the sales process involves considerations dealing with customization or configuration, or when guidance is needed in evaluating what to buy, the value in the sales experience takes center stage.

The collective insight and expertise your company brings to the table becomes the difference between winning and losing. It's your opportunity to help customers think differently about the issues they are facing and how you may be able to help them, in the same way that Garry helped me to see a different approach to cooling my house. Customers come to companies all the time with an idea of what they want to buy. But when there are multifaceted decisions to be made about the solution that is best for them or the way it would be most effectively implemented, the sales experience can help to drive better decisions, more effective implementations, and stronger customer outcomes and results.

A sales organization whose role is to create this kind of valuable sales experience and a sales team who has been read into the company strategy are positioned to create value by introducing customers to ideas for doing new things or for doing old things better.

A few years ago, I was working with an editor at a prestigious business publication for an article on this topic. His take was that there was nothing new here; it was just the same old solution selling. This frustrated me to no end, because he shared the same blind spot as so many leaders who fail to leverage the sales experience as a differentiator. I took that as my cue to do a better job of explaining what was, in fact, so very different. Sure, the basic skills involved are much the same and have been part of sales training programs for decades. But the way they are applied, the way organizations prioritize the sales experience, and the way they are a part of a strategic effort—rather than only being the focus for a few days of training on sales technique—make all the difference.

Solution selling is one of the many synonyms of *consultative selling*. And every business in the market claims to sell solutions. But the truth is that a so-called solution is not really a solution until it solves something for a customer. That requires a direct connection to the outcomes that a customer wants to achieve—their objectives to be accomplished, their problems to be solved, their needs to be addressed—by buying your products and services and accessing your support. Until that is agreed upon with a customer, your solutions aren't yet solutions. A solution is not so much created by a strategically informed seller as it is cocreated by that seller and the customer in a mutual agreement about the business outcomes to be achieved. Such cocreation happens in one place and one place only: the sales experience. Sales calls that deliver such a sales experience are calls that a customer will pay for, and they will willingly pay for the experience again and again. Most of all, when you win the sales experience, everything else gets a little easier, from price negotiations to repeat business.

I worked with the executives and sales team at a maintenance, repair, and operations (MRO) supply company that sold all kinds of parts, equipment, and supplies in the heavy manufacturing market. One of the thousands of products they sold were V-clips, often called alligator clips. In this case, they were being sold to a purchasing manager in an automotive manufacturing plant. The clips were being used to hang and ground auto parts as they moved through an electrostatic paint line in the plant.

In the MRO world, there is intense price pressure on the category of non-product-related items. These are items used during the production process that are not part of the company's finished goods or products. Rather than engage as a purveyor of clips and dig into negotiations on price for the components, the sales team focused on the customer's outcomes instead of the parts themselves.

Taking a more strategic approach allowed a deeper dialogue that included the director of operations for the plant. The sales team helped the buyers understand the dire consequences of going with the lower-cost clips. Those cheaper clips could save them tens of thousands of dollars, but anytime one of them broke, it could shut down their production line for hours at a time. And being shut down would cost them $1.2 million per hour.

A broken clip can turn into hours and hours of downtime while employees fix the problem. Factor in the costs of staff-related overtime and missed delivery deadlines, and those clips, incidental in size and not even a part of the final product, had a major impact. So, when the sellers from the MRO company proposed clips that cost nearly three times more than the clips they were currently using, the decision was not difficult; it was a solution to an important issue. This solution was cocreated in the sales experience with the buyers. The win came because the sales experience for a commodity product was about risk, not about price.

The highest and best use for the sales organization is to create value by bringing the go-to-market strategy to life in every one of their sales calls. After all, it is in the sales call that your employees connect with current and prospective clients to determine whether you will win or lose in the market. This, in turn, requires acting on the urgent need to sell things differently—that is, to create a compelling sales experience. The sales organization must sell in ways that go beyond merely articulating the value of a product, service, or capabilities. Sellers need to offer genuine solutions that help clients achieve their objectives. A sales call that creates value in this way wins a sale that differentiates your company's value proposition from those of others by presenting your company as a partner committed to offering an effective solution, not just unloading a widget.

One of my mentors used to say that "if you want to know how sellers ought to sell, learn how buyers buy." With the sales experience as a central part of your strategy, having a well-defined approach to where and how you create value becomes of critical importance. A sales experience that creates value executes strategy rather than killing it. When I talk to executives about sales in these terms, they understand, yet they also recognize that selling differently to create value is not common practice. After all, shedding the baggage of the status quo is rarely easy.

FLAG 5: WHERE MUST WE IMPROVE, BUILD, OR ACQUIRE TO EXECUTE OUR STRATEGY?

I found myself frustrated by something an executive once said to me. He had just been washed out as CEO by the board of directors because his transformation strategy failed to produce results.

"Scott," he muttered to me over breakfast, "I *know* we had a great strategy, but we failed with the sales team and execution."

It reminded me of that old quip about the surgeon who delivers the bad news to an anxious family: "The operation was a success, but the patient died." The idea that strategy can fail in execution but still be a great strategy is a fundamental misunderstanding of what strategy is. Prior to execution, any strategy is inert, nonliving. At most, it is a spore, encased in its shell. It comes to life and lives only in its implementation. As Roger L. Martin, former Rotman School of Management dean and a renowned expert on strategy, wrote in the *Harvard Business Review*, the notion that execution is distinct from strategy is essentially flawed. The purpose of a strategy, he wrote, "is to generate positive results . . . In what other field do we proclaim something to be brilliant that has failed miserably . . . ? The only strategy that can legitimately be called brilliant is one whose results are exemplary. A strategy that fails to produce a great outcome is simply a failure."[10]

Any strategy that fails to include within itself the elements necessary for its own execution is a failed strategy. If the strategy of your enterprise does not include a direct line of sight from top leadership to the rest of the organization, and especially the sales organization, it is a failed strategy.

The fifth and final signal of our Five Flag Start shifts gear from projecting your future and begins to address how to ensure that desired future will be realized. That is—what will you do to execute your strategy and how will you do it? I often describe flag 5 as the bridge to execution. It expresses what you must do to make your strategy real. You will not achieve your strategy by declaration. And you've likely seen plenty of strategies fail because they lacked an element of pragmatism that defines what the company must do in order to make the strategy a success.

The first four flags outline the components of an effective strategy. They are the framework of an aspiration, since a strategy is something not yet achieved. This is where the fifth flag comes in. In asking, "What must we improve, build, or acquire to execute the strategy successfully?" the fifth flag is about what is needed to transform aspiration into action. The fifth flag shows the way to make the first four flags real. It is about getting clear on what needs to happen. What do you need to do—that won't just happen in the course of running your business—to make that strategy come to life? Answer this question with precision and clarity, and you will have a road map that defines the work to be done in execution.

To execute your strategy, there are probably some things you do now that you need to be better at: selling, marketing, manufacturing, supply chain management, and so on. You have to improve the way you are doing these functions to compete the way this strategy says you will. And there are probably some things you need that you don't have today. Maybe you need to develop innovative capabilities or services, modernize an approach for R&D, or establish management practices for growth. Maybe you need a new distribution channel like direct sales, resellers, or online sales. Or maybe you need systems to support scaling for growth, like enterprise resource planning or financial systems or CRM. And if you can't build these things, you need to go get them. Buy them or partner with someone to deliver them.

The Five Flag Start is a way of ensuring that the decision to execute a given strategy is based on facts that are established as objectively as possible. Get to the point at which you can wave all five flags, and you can, with confidence, declare yourself ready to execute your strategy to drive growth. Your entire organization will be revved up to achieve your revenue goals. And you'll be able to effect positive and intentional change. The Five Flag Start marks a series of choices that guide the nature and direction of your business. The flags are instruments for achieving the crisp, concise, clear, and precise focus needed to execute a strategy effectively and unequivocally. Everyone who sees these flags will recognize what is happening, where they are going, and what they need to do.

CHAPTER 5

Right by Three

People are, of course, what make your business go. And culture determines how all those people work together to make your business grow.

Jim Collins introduced one of the most popular concepts in business over the last twenty-five years: "Get the right people on the bus." The idea is that, if you focus on "first who then what,"[1] as he writes, no matter what chaos or uncertainty your business faces, no matter the challenges, you'll be facing it all with the right people in the right seats. After all, who wouldn't want to take on the greatest challenges in your business with all the right people? But unless you are starting a brand-new organization and starting to recruit a brand-new team tomorrow, you already have a company bus full of people in assigned seats. So, it's challenging to focus on first who then what, since you need to do both simultaneously while your bus is already moving fast.

I expanded Collins's list by one and went deeper to illustrate how to apply his idea to leading growth. I call this approach *Right by Three*, meaning you have to be right in all three areas if you are to be ready to lead for growth.

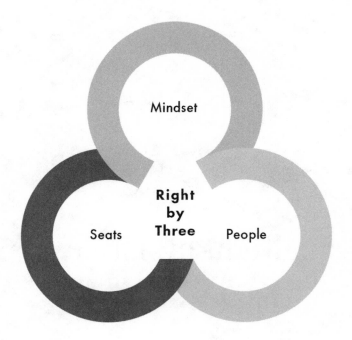

RIGHT BY THREE

- The right mindset

- The right people

- The right seats at the table

THE RIGHT MINDSET

In many ways I've talked a lot about mindset so far in this book, particularly in how Growth Leaders think about strategy, leadership, and sales. But let's take a moment here to crystallize the right mindset for growth.

When everyone in the company shares a common set of beliefs that lead to behaviors, we call that the company's *culture*. This is not to say people don't think on their own or that there is never disagreement. But broadly, a shared set of beliefs about how we are intended to act, how we operate as a group, and what we expect from each other and from our performance determine what is acceptable within any organization.

Those beliefs exist about seemingly small things, like how we think about being on time to meetings. In some organizations, being even a minute late is considered unacceptable, while in others, trickling into a meeting or joining a videoconference a couple of minutes late goes unnoticed. And they exist about big things like how we think about customers. I worked with an organization where the unstated but overriding belief among the engineering and manufacturing teams was that customers were typically wrong about how they wanted to approach projects. The requests they made were more of a nuisance than an important consideration. You can imagine the problems that arise in contentious customer relationships when that is the starting point.

A strongly ingrained set of shared beliefs necessarily establishes the standards of behavior and expectations for performance. These beliefs may be explicit or implicit, written or unwritten, and most of all, intentional or unintentional. But every organization has them.

Sometimes the real beliefs within an organization are different from those that are stated by its leaders. This is, no doubt, the thorniest challenge of building or changing culture. That kind of dissonance creates all manner of problems with trust, productivity, and results. That's why it is so vital that executives keep a close eye on the elements of culture that are most important for their business. You must be aware of the beliefs that are most useful in encouraging and fostering the behaviors that you want to see in your organization.

To build a growth-focused culture, there are necessarily beliefs about the sales organization and the role of sales for your business that deserve your attention. By now, you may have started to question some of those beliefs that have been influenced by antiquated thinking about sales and its strategic role in the growth of your business. To that end, here are some of the beliefs that will help you instill the right mindset for growth. Starting with the CEO and executive team, these beliefs work their way through the organization.

- Company differentiation is a combination of what we sell and how we sell it.

- The sales experience is a part of our competitive advantage.

- The sales function leads the execution of our strategy in the market; every sales call reflects the success or failure of our strategy.

- Sales roles require considerable professional skill and expertise to bring value to customers.

- Leading the sales function requires excellent strategic perspective and the ability to develop talent.

These beliefs inform dozens upon dozens of decisions and choices about how the sales organization fits into the larger organization as a critical driver of growth. They inform who you recruit, how you compensate, how you manage, how you align with strategy, how you drive collaboration and teamwork with marketing, and so forth.

You'll recall the common belief that sales is a job that "anyone can do."[2] Well, if that is a prevailing belief in your company, it is likely that you'll be recruiting, managing, developing, and compensating in sync with that belief. It will mean you focus mostly on personality traits like charisma or extroversion and ignoring the skills that are most likely to make someone successful in consultative selling today, like problem solving and critical thinking skills.

In the same vein, that belief is often connected to the idea that salespeople need to be hungry or possess a fire in the belly. How do you imagine the sales experience with that person? Does it seem like they are interested in helping you address the issues that are most important to you and providing you with value? I sometimes ask executives who tell me that they believe this is one of the most important characteristics for a salesperson, "When was the last time you had a good sales experience with someone who was hungry or trying to close you?" I think you'll agree that it's not a pleasant customer experience.

Another commonly held belief is that sales professionals are coin operated, primarily motivated by money. If that is who you look for, then that is who you will find. There are plenty of transactional sellers you can recruit that will fall right in line with that belief. And leaders often choose to use compensation as a substitute for management and leadership, believing that they just need their people to be more driven, to push harder, and to sell more.

But this poor substitute for leadership won't get you very far. Compensation may help you get more effort or a different area of focus, but it will not make your sales team better. It may drive some to work harder or more hours. It may incentivize a particular focus on a new product or solution. But it will not make your sellers better at selling those solutions. It will not make them more able to use your company's expertise to help customers think differently about issues and consider your solutions. I've often joked that you could pay me $1 million to dunk a basketball in a year. I may put in a great deal of effort and try incredibly hard, but I'm unlikely to shatter any backboards (though I might shatter a knee).

But none of these characteristics will help you win in the market. On the other hand, when there is a cultural belief that the sales role requires a level of specialized expertise, it drives different recruiting behaviors as you seek to attract intelligence and problem-solving skills, the tools needed to execute strategy. You make different decisions about compensation and motivation with a more strategic role in mind.

Plenty of these beliefs run counter to the way sales is imagined in many organizations, whether from outdated stereotypes that die hard or simply a lack of contemporary understanding. When it comes to leading growth, if a material portion of your revenue comes through a channel that requires sellers to meet with customers and prospects, these beliefs are critical parts of the right mindset. This mindset, starting with the CEO and executive team, creates the culture that allows your sales organization to thrive as part of the value-creating engine of your business.

In most organizations, beliefs are deliberately represented in a set of values, but even if they're not overtly connected, the values are clues to the beliefs that underlie the organization's behavior. Optimally, the beliefs and values that create culture are positively differentiating—particularly when people know them and understand how they are visible within a company.

Most company values are good ones. Things like respect for others, accountability, innovation, customer commitment, collaboration, and integrity are obviously beneficial. In fact, if we were to make a list of the top fifty corporate values, we'd add things like transparency, a focus on results, operational excellence, enthusiasm, and so many more. They may be expressed as just these terms, or they may be written as more action-oriented statements, but none of them would be bad. Most importantly for you, as a Growth Leader, most any set of company values can support your efforts to drive growth.

Too often, however, company values are, at best, an afterthought. I frequently ask leaders at all levels in organizations to state their company's values. Rarely can they tell me all of them, which undoubtedly means that these values do not drive daily behavior in the organization.

An important step toward more intentionally crafting a growth-focused culture is identifying the beliefs that will drive the desired behaviors in your company. Those behaviors are capable of unlocking results and delivering value in everything the company does, including the sales experience. And if your company already has values in place, then you can work with them to illustrate for everyone what they look like in action.

One highly effective set of beliefs that drives culture-building behaviors is offered by Bendcare, a healthcare company that specializes in helping rheumatologists standardize and simplify their practices with improved access, advocacy, technology, training, and education. I worked with the company to develop a set of what CEO and chairman Andrew Ripps calls *A+ values*, a term we used interchangeably with beliefs.

When Andrew and I started working together, he came to me and said, "I want to build a culture of high performance, a culture that will support exponential growth." The values were already in place, and people were aware of them, but Andrew and his executive team's effort to dig in and define what these values and beliefs looked like in action made the difference in their success. Their purpose was to drive the key behaviors that create a growth-focused culture. These behaviors would be coached, managed, recognized, and rewarded so they became vivid for everyone in the organization. Each A+ value is associated with a set of behaviors:

BE AUTHENTIC

- Deliver and create innovative and personalized simple solutions.

- Restore control to both the physician and the patient.

- Listen attentively to our colleagues when they are speaking.

- Avoid cutting people out or off when sharing their perspectives.

- Focus on behaviors, circumstances, and issues, not the person.

- Use email as a last resort. Video or in-person communication is more valuable.

- Avoid multitasking when we are in meetings or during conversation.

- Don't surprise a colleague with bad or important news in public.

BE ACCOUNTABLE

- Confirm understanding of our commitments.

- Set clear expectations.

- Collaborate to identify best options to achieve our common goal.

- Follow up and prioritize actions in a timely manner.

- Assign responsibility to one owner, who is the subject-matter expert.

- Learn fast from the undesired outcome and implement the learning to accomplish future goals.

BE ADAPTABLE

- Have the courage to ask why we are doing it this way.

- Always look for new and creative ways while thinking objectively.

- Solicit feedback and welcome it nondefensively.

- Commit to understanding insights from our colleagues on continuous improvement.

- Course-correct based on new information.

- Identify the cause, not blame, when mistakes are made.

- Escalate critical information to your direct report quickly to course-correct or solve a problem.

BE APPRECIATIVE

- Never miss an opportunity to recognize someone's contribution and performance.

- Thank others for both effort and results.

- Recognize others when they exhibit behavior in living our values.

- Offer support to colleagues when in need or facing difficult times.

- Operate with pride in everything you do.

Andrew Ripps and his leadership team enumerate the desired behaviors very specifically, but this precision is not to be confused with micromanagement. Translating beliefs into behaviors is the way that an organization's culture is created. Beliefs are ideas, behaviors are actions, and culture is the context in which strategy gains meaning and becomes capable of execution. This is not micromanagement; it is leadership.

Creating a successful culture requires that leaders at every level of the enterprise articulate the organization's beliefs, identify the behaviors to enact the beliefs, and model those behaviors by practicing them. Because behaviors are actions, not abstractions, they are concrete, visible, and subject to observation and straightforward evaluation. You can see what works, what needs improvement, and what does not work at all.

Ripps begins by articulating his company's mission and vision. He says their mission is to "design, deliver, and discover quality in specialty medicine that dictates the formula for safe, cost-effective, and patient-centric outcomes." Ripps goes on to explain the company vision, which is to focus on the patient and make "healthcare healthier through our delivery of services, technology, education, and purchase power solutions that improve the patient experience, care, and value."[3]

The belief is in the value and validity of this mission and this vision, which can be transformed from aspiration to achievement by behaviors that are authentic, accountable, adaptable, and appreciative. Bendcare's leadership attaches those specific behaviors—actions—listed above to each category and works with key people throughout the company to develop each behavior.

Those key people are role models, the hidden leaders that can be found at every level of the organization. They may or may not have titles that place them high up on an org chart. Their leadership does not depend on a title. It comes from modeling what you want to see in the organization. A successful growth-focused culture starts at the top, with the CEO and other C-suite leaders. Nothing can substitute for this level of leadership in shaping culture. Nevertheless, leadership, by definition, cannot be a solo act. A leader needs followers, of course, but in a complex business organization, at least some of those followers must also be capable of influencing others. Social media calls them influencers.

In a business organization, the C-suite needs to be diligent and intentional about identifying and leveraging its hidden leaders. As Laurie Sain and I explained in *The Hidden Leader: Discover and Develop Greatness within Your Company*, "You and others have called these workers smart, crucial, effective, or an important part of the company. You have seen them work effectively with people at many levels within the organization, from front lines to executive suites, regardless of their formal positions. But if you thought at all about these employees' abilities, you probably categorized them as having natural talent that couldn't be replicated." You may not have seen them as leaders, but they are leaders, and they're "sources of great strategic advantage in your company," and "they can be defined, identified, nurtured, and encouraged to help an organization develop a competitive edge."[4]

In their behavior, the hidden leaders in any organization amplify strategic messages of belief and value so that they echo throughout the company. They weave the web of behaviors into a culture. But they're not the only ones. The behaviors that create a culture cannot be dictated to the organization. They must be modeled. The talk can be talked, but walking the walk matters most. Your entire team is watching you, listening to what you say. You have enormous power to shape your company's culture.

An executive who communicates openly, thoughtfully, and courteously, who invites questions and discussion and feedback, who listens actively and attentively, and who handles conflict with firmness leavened by grace and understanding, provides a model for dealing with colleagues, subordinates, and customers alike. Add to this unwavering honesty, an alignment of words with actions, a willingness to admit mistakes, a practice of consistently following through on promises, and you have a demonstration of a respectful, ethical culture. You have built a basis for trust.

Growth-focused culture requires the long view

If you want to see long-term results, you need to see short-term progress. But too many leaders confuse progress with results. It takes some time to shift behavior in organizations consistently, and then it takes time for those behaviors to yield the fruit of results. Apply that across a business, and establishing culture requires a short and long view: driving the right actions and behaviors in the short term and the patience to see those actions create results in the long term.

Results, like increases in revenue, higher Net Promoter Scores, expanded margins, and net income growth, tend to take some time to show up. You won't be ready to run a marathon after a few weeks of running. But it won't happen at all if you don't start with a few weeks of running and build on them.

As James Clear writes in *Atomic Habits*, "It is so easy to overestimate the importance of one defining moment and underestimate the value of making small improvements on a daily basis."[5] Clear popularized the success of the British Cycling team as they went from a century of mediocrity to a dominant force in the cycling world, winning more than half the gold medals in the 2008 Olympics and winning five of six Tours de France from 2012 to 2017. The right mindset for the British Cycling team was instilled by new coach Sir Dave Brailsford, who was committed to a strategy he referred to as "the aggregation of marginal gains." This philosophy involved searching for a tiny margin of improvement in everything you do. Clear quotes Brailsford as saying, "The whole principle came from the idea that if you broke down everything you could think of that goes into riding a bike, and then improve it by 1 percent, you will get a significant increase when you put them all together."[6] It's compound interest at work. Collecting small gains, by every person in your company, every day, is what drives longer-term results.

To be sure, there are plenty of CEOs who develop long-term strategies for the companies they lead. But even these often latch on to areas in which they see opportunity for short-term gains. An overfocus on controlling expenses is one such area, since cost cutting is typically expedient, producing relatively rapid results. When you cut costs today, the reduction may start to show up as early as next month's P&L. To be sure, I'm always in favor of effectively controlling expenses. And your business model needs to be rational or your company won't exist for long. Just understand that no company ever achieves their business objectives by focusing primarily on cutting costs. It can produce a near-term gain for the bottom line. But without a balanced view of the impact on your ability to drive positive results with customers and to invest in the resources needed to win in the market, doing so won't likely help you execute your strategy and achieve success. A chief financial officer at a Fortune 500 company I worked with used to call this the "cut and shrink" death spiral. She recognized the pattern of rolling cost reductions and how they impacted the company's ability to grow. You can only cut a cost once, and then it's done and gone. You can only eliminate a job once. You can only "optimize" in this way just so much. Of course, there may be moments where the company belt may need to tighten. That's reality. But going too far, as they say, cutting beyond the fat, into the muscle of the company or even to the bone, endangers your ability to lead growth. So, be sure you do a really good job—the *first* time—with the scalpel or the cleaver. And then move on to growth.

Many leaders reflexively look to sales for another source of short-term gains. Unfortunately, revenue and profit take far longer than reducing costs. Consider the length of your sales cycles and the time it takes to identify and attract customers to engage in those sales cycles.

Author Geoffrey Moore, best known for his books *Crossing the Chasm* and *Zone to Win*, references the financial concept of the J-curve to illustrate how investing heavily in a new strategy can take time to yield results. As a company sinks money into developing a new business model, there is a sharp drop in profits, which eventually becomes a steep upward trajectory as the new offering successfully comes online. One of the main obstacles in transformation efforts is not being able to, as Moore writes, "stomach the J-curve."[7] A big risk is bailing out too soon on a growth strategy and losing out on both the investment and any substantive future return. During Microsoft's digital transformation efforts, as the company moved from primarily providing hardware to a subscription cloud-based model, there was an initial period of low revenues and high investment costs. Satya Nadella understood and was able to manage the J-curve.

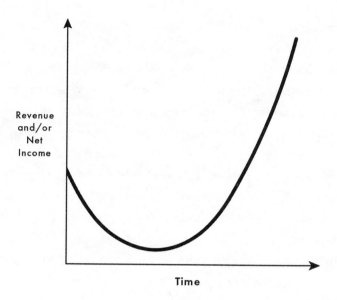

Sacrificing long-term investments to deliver quarterly earnings has long been identified as a management affliction. In his valuable review on short-termism published in *Harvard Business Review*, Roger L. Martin points out that cost reduction is often a CEO response to relentless investment market pressure for short-term performance. Martin cites a study in which 80 percent of four hundred large US company CFOs interviewed said they "would sacrifice economic value for the firm in order to meet that quarter's earnings expectations." Shocking as this is, Martin suspects that, in reality, the number "is closer to 100 percent."[8]

For a Growth Leader, the pressure can create a challenging situation. As Martin explains, markets are relentless in their demands for quarterly profit growth. And executives respond logically to this pressure—they buy back stock and strangle investments in long-term growth. This causes low top-line growth. The executives are then punished by the markets, which tell them that "they won't be able to maintain profit growth without revenue growth. Duh! Of course! You reap what you sow."[9]

But more frequently the call is coming from inside the house. A great deal of the pressure created comes from the C-suite themselves. The authors of a more recent *Harvard Business Review* article take on the claim from CEOs that they have to give in to the demands of Wall Street and others to regularly boost quarterly profits. The authors point out that most of the pressure, in fact, comes from within the company, from its own board and its own executive team, from a combination of different self-interests and shortsighted goals, which are antithetical to being a Growth Leader. The article argues that "CEOs shouldn't be putting so much pressure on themselves to get strong short-term results" but should look to the example of "a small and growing number of forward-thinking CEOs [who] are putting the long-term health of their companies ahead of boosting short-term profits."[10]

Focusing on the sales experience as part of the company's competitive advantage is not just a sales strategy; it is a corporate strategy executed by the sales organization for long-term growth. But even if your company made this change completely in the next week and your sales organization was fully ready to deliver a valuable sales experience on every sales call, perfectly executing your strategy, it would still take some time for the results to show up. Of course, there would be some immediate and short-term successes and wins. But if your average sales cycle is four months or six months or longer, as are many in the B2B world, then that is likely about as fast as the result will be seen on the scoreboard. This requires an investment in the capabilities of the sales team, in recruitment, development, compensation, and career—an investment in your people.

THE RIGHT PEOPLE

Do a search of leadership competency models, and you'll find hundreds of options, most of them at least good. In many cases, I find that too many of these models are exercises in renaming the periodic table. What one calls *character*, another calls *trust building* or *integrity* or *honesty*. While some put massive survey and data analysis and rigor into it (and we'll leverage that where it is available), it's not often revelatory. In our *Harvard Business Review* article "Making Yourself Indispensable," which was based on research on more than 25,000 leaders, Jack Zenger, Joe Folkman, and I discovered that *powerful and broad communication* is one of the differentiating competencies that separates excellent leaders from their average counterparts. We identified a total of sixteen, such as strategic perspective, interpersonal skills, and driving for results. In the original research, it was listed as *powerful and prolific communication*, and when I'd talk with clients, they really liked that characterization; it is absolutely useful to understand that we are talking about more than basic skill levels when it comes to high-performance leadership. But it wasn't as if we discovered plutonium or something. It's fairly obvious that excellent communication skills are an important part of leading. Like values, it is hard to find a leadership competency that doesn't reflect a desirable quality. The real key is being able to put the ideas into action and pragmatically apply leadership competencies to achieve your specific goals. When I coach executives on how they will grow their business, we routinely look for how particular leadership skills can be activated to help them reach their objectives. For the Growth Leader, a handful of skills are essential for you as well as your team.

One afternoon, I made a request of Joe Folkman, who ran all of our analysis as one of the world's leading psychometricians. As part of a project we were working on, our client was interested in which competencies were most characteristic of the top sales leaders in the Zenger Folkman database. We compared the results of the sales leadership data with the data from leaders of other functions and came up with a set of six competencies most valuable to leading sales growth:

- Strategic perspective

- Focus on results

- Inspires and motivates others to high performance

- Powerful and prolific communication

- Teamwork and collaboration

- Developing others

It's easy to see how these competencies would enable leaders to drive the growth of their business.

Taking this idea further, McKinsey & Company partnered with Egon Zehnder International to examine the relationship between growth and specific leadership traits.[11] Reviewing data, the researchers identified the eight core leadership competencies found in top-performing companies. They demonstrated a direct correlation between leaders who exhibit these competencies and revenue growth for the company:

- Market insight

- Strategic orientation

- Developing organizational capability

- Change leadership

- Team leadership

- Collaboration and influencing

- Customer impact

- Results orientation

I was struck by how closely these eight items harmonize with the six competencies our own research revealed. The themes were eerily similar, and four of the six were nearly identical.

Plenty of combinations of leadership skills contribute to growth, and the necessary leadership competencies vary considerably, depending on the company strategy. But no leadership competency was as important to the growth of a business as customer impact. There was an incredibly strong correlation between a company's revenue growth and its C-suite leaders' effectiveness with customers. The same correlation was true for the senior management group below the executives on the organization chart. To be a Growth Leader, customer impact is a must.

A little bit of synthesis of all this research can help you, as a Growth Leader, to identify and develop the right people.

Putting the customer at the center

All of your revenue comes from customers, so you'd better know a lot about them. Head and shoulders, this is more significant than any other leadership competency for making a difference for leaders to drive growth. And I'd suspect that this is the biggest weakness of CEOs coming from finance and operations, which seems to be the case in most big companies.

A customer focus requires understanding how the sales organization—your company's lifeline connection to the customer—creates value in the sales process. You must prioritize designing and delivering a compelling sales experience with insight, expertise, and perspective. And a Growth Leader knows how the entire organization supports the sales experience and (if the sales experience goes well) the customer experience. It is vital to understand the contemporary reality of the decades-old idea of consultative sales and what it takes for the sales organization to do it well. You must also understand the reality for sales, the market challenges they face, the issues customers are struggling with, and why customers choose competitors over you.

A focus on strategy

Having a strategy and being clear about that strategy are critical to success. Part of this is understanding all areas of your business and how you compete and win in the market. Strategy, as I speak about it, is the clarity brought about by the Five Flag Start. It is crucial to clearly identify your ideal client profile, to detail your specific advantages and the reasons your clients will choose you over the competition, and to clarify the customer issues that will likely drive them toward that decision. The fifth flag (build, improve, acquire) highlights the chance to fill gaps to support the strategy. Sales is the execution of strategy. Ultimately, every sales call reflects the success or failure of your strategy. It is critical to make the go-to-market strategy precise so that it influences all sales actions. This is how you use your strategy to influence every customer relationship in the company.

Leading for results

Measures like revenue or net income are the ultimate scoreboard, the ultimate result. There are plenty of other important results as well, so if your entire team is not focused properly on the outcomes, your strategy can go awry. A focus on results requires a thoughtful consideration of the work that needs to be done to ensure the business can deliver. This is the fifth flag of the Five Flag Start again. This is not only about achieving numbers but ensuring that the initiatives and resources are in place to deliver on the sales experience we want to create. The results orientation necessarily includes the ability to execute, the process to get results. The Growth Leader must understand and ensure that the organization has the resources, systems, people, processes, and coaching and development to drive revenue. This means investing in building capability and strength and creating a high-performance organization. This is the opposite of just saying, "Get out and sell or produce more." It isn't simply demanding results or the sort of annoying myopic focus of incessantly asking about numbers. It's leading, organizing, planning, and marshaling the resources your team needs so you can get the results you need to grow.

The ability to inspire and motivate others

The executive sets the strategy and collaborates in defining the work to be done. But then it's got to be executed by everyone. Being able to inspire and connect with people to build enthusiasm and drive the business forward is a crucial skill not only for the CEO but for all the leaders in your organization. For a leader to inspire, they must have a practical approach to using emotion, of genuinely connecting with people. They must be a strong communicator who provides a clear message, no equivocation, no bullshit or corporate speak. They must invest in others, developing their talents and spending time to help them grow. All this builds loyalty, so you get the discretionary effort. And of course, they must be visionary. Great strategy is crucial, but having some vision that is exciting about what we could be, what we are capable of, what we all stand to gain, why it's so cool that we have the chance to do this . . . that's what inspiration is all about.

A focus on development

As a business aims to grow, one of the most critical capabilities you need is the skill required to bring your strategy to life. It can be tempting to hand anything under the umbrella of talent development to the HR function, since they typically deal with development. But it would be a mistake to leave building this vital capability exclusively to HR. With no disrespect to HR, they can provide support and resources, but it takes a leader to make something an organizational priority.

Development and coaching ought to be viewed as an executive imperative to fuel growth, with leaders at all levels concentrating a part of their attention on improving the skills of their teams. Most important among these competencies are the leadership and customer-facing skills that help teams compete more effectively, create value, and build loyalty. These skills aren't easily learned in training programs, and they certainly aren't learned in school. Development programs can be useful, but nothing creates sustained behavioral change in people like coaching from their leaders. Skills must be honed and developed on the job, in the context of that job.

There is a direct correlation between leadership effectiveness and business performance, specifically with net income growth, employee turnover, increased revenue, productivity, and more.[12] Depending on which studies you look at, sales managers can improve a seller's performance by 20 percent or more.[13] This doesn't happen by sending people to a series of courses. It occurs when executives recognize that developing talent in the organization is a critical leadership responsibility and get serious about it as a criterion for evaluating performance, considering promotion, and even determining compensation. That's where a culture of coaching and developing others to reach high levels of performance begins to take hold.

Change leadership

Maintaining the status quo doesn't require a lot of leadership, and growth is inevitably about change. Having the skill to lead through transformation is key. Not only the CEO but the entire leadership team must be Growth Leaders, using all their abilities to describe the current state of the company as a step toward the desired future state. To bring your team along, you must vividly express what the change looks like for your way of attracting and developing client relationships and then describe the steps along the way, the milestones of progress. Once your team understands what the change looks like, then you must be able to put in place the systems (with a results focus) that are required to implement that vision, dealing with adversity and roadblocks, losses, and setbacks along the way.

Collaboration and influence

Companies are typically organized by functions, which often become silos. But customers do not interact with or experience your company as silos. They experience you as a company, not customer service or tech support or sales in isolation; whoever is interacting with the customer is the face of your company. So, connectivity among all functions—whether they produce your products and services or provide them to customers—is crucial. Being a Growth Leader requires you to collaborate with all the functions of your business to build the synergy required to win and retain customers.

Most managers will advance in their careers by leading vertically: tending to what the boss requests, fostering connection with the supervisor, and managing direct reports and the levels beneath them in their function. Everyone else is a colleague, but the main attention goes to strengthening relationships and collaborating up and down the functional team. Growth leadership requires a horizontal approach to teamwork. It requires the ability to influence the actions of others through the power of relationships and expertise rather than simply directing others. As you lead growth by attracting and developing the right kind of customers, you need to foster teamwork between marketing and sales, fueled by collaboration toward common goals rather than their usual narrow functional focus. The same is true in driving alignment on your strategy from all functions, creating connections across the business in the service of your strategy.

THE RIGHT SEATS AT THE TABLE

Peter Drucker, who I think of as the GOAT of management consultants, said, "The purpose of business [is] to create a customer."[14] Let's apply Drucker's insight about creating a customer to what I count as the three primary business functions:

- Make or deliver something

- Sell it

- Collect and manage money for doing these things

Planning and executing these functions calls, in turn, for leadership in three corresponding areas:

- Operations

- Sales

- Finance

There are plenty of other activities and functions to support doing these things well, and operations often consists of an incredibly wide range of actions. Operations can include everything from researching and innovating to designing to building and fulfilling whatever it is you provide for customers. Of course, all functions believe they are the most important.

But if we accept the fact that you have to sell something in order to consider anyone a customer, then selling is surely one primary business function, and the executive roundtable needs a seat for sales. As a participant in strategic conversations, a sales leader will directly influence the thinking about achievable objectives, the resources required to compete more effectively, and the barriers to overcome so that growth may be accelerated or sustained. You need to have people in the right seats at your roundtable.

Nobody knows whether Britain's King Arthur was a man of flesh and blood or strictly of myth. But one of his most celebrated legends is seating his knights at a roundtable. The point of the roundtable is that it has no single *point*. It is a circle, on whose circumference all points are equally important—a great message for inclusion of everyone's perspective. Part of the struggle is that, depending on what you read, at the low end, his table had maybe a dozen seats for various knights; at the high end, perhaps 1,600. That would require a table about four times the size of a football field. Fortunately, the executive team is nowhere that size, but the increase of C-suite positions in recent years makes it nearly impossible for all to have an equal voice on decisions of strategy. A *Wall Street Journal* headline screamed in agony: "The Proliferation of C-suite Titles Is Insane!" Yahoo!'s security director was officially titled "paranoid-in-chief,"[15] and *Forbes* published an article titled "C Is for Silly," highlighting major companies with leaders holding titles like *chief joy officer*. Not counting the laughable titles, you see companies with ten or more C-level positions. There is a healthy dose of title inflation here, which isn't in and of itself an issue. Call them all CXO. But the fact remains that you need a smaller, more focused group of leaders driving the most important results in your business.

That's why it's important to come back to Drucker's formulation about a business enterprise existing to create a customer, and to organize your leadership roundtable with the right seats to prioritize that as a primary objective. As Drucker further states, "Marketing and innovation produce results; all the rest are costs."[16] Broaden that insight a little bit to determine what functions are vital and should have seats at your roundtable.

More often than not, sales leadership doesn't have a prominent role in strategic involvement with the CEO and the executive team. Two common problems keep organizations from adding a proper seat for sales:

- There is not enough sales in leadership.

- There is not enough leadership in sales.

It may be too late for you to solve the first problem. But you're lucky: Solving the other one will also solve the first one for you.

Not enough sales in leadership

Bob Dutkowsky, now the chairman of the board of US Foods, said it clearly when he referenced the aphorism known as Miles' law during one of our conversations:

> Where you stand on issues depends on where you sit. Too often, I see CEOs who come from manufacturing, operations, finance, and so forth who don't properly value the role of sales in executing strategy. They think they just need to build something great and tell the sales team to just go and *sell*. In other words, *just go and pitch*.
>
> CEOs who came up through customer-facing roles—or at least have a strong understanding of what it takes to be successful in a modern selling environment—understand that it is sales that must connect our products and solutions to the needs, wants, and problems of our current and prospective customers.
>
> It's the sales team that must understand what customers are trying to achieve, what they want to accomplish, and why

THEY WIN. With this understanding, sales connects customers to the products and services we can provide. That is
what drives the execution of your company's strategy—in the
field, every day.

The C-suite bias against sales, I believe, comes in large part from the
stigma surrounding sales and the limited sales experience of most CEOs. A
small percentage of major company CEOs arrived in the C-suite through
sales. It may be the least represented major function. You don't have to have
come from sales to lead growth, but you must understand what is required
to make sales successful.

Not enough leadership in sales

Among the most common reasons the leader of the sales team, whatever
title they wear, is not a part of the inner circle of their company is that they
are not a seasoned enough business leader. There are plenty of extraordinary
leaders of sales organizations. But more often than not, the leader of the sales
organization is not as experienced or seasoned as the leaders of the other
primary functions.

The odds are in our favor that this person started as a sales rep and has
been promoted steadily to bigger and bigger sales leadership jobs. On the
surface, that may seem fine. But given the arm's-length relationship sales
tends to have with the CEO and the rest of the executives, the sales leader
is not typically involved in a meaningful way with anything but sales. That
silo limits their growth and development as leaders and keeps them from
providing a broader contribution to the business. Contrast that with leaders
in finance or operations, who must have a deeper understanding of the rest
of the business. Sales leaders are also far more likely to be in the field with
their team and with customers than circulating internally. Add these factors together, and it's not hard to see why sales leadership is on the outside
looking in.

Where other functional leaders continue to grow as executives, collaborating across functions and addressing organization-wide problems, sales leaders—from the time they are first managers until they reach VP or EVP—are focused almost exclusively on sales alone. While their function is critically important and requires high levels of skill and specialization, it keeps them out of higher-profile leadership opportunities. As a result, sales is not seated with much frequency at the executive roundtable, where strategy is formulated and revised.

What seat is right?

At the jerk of a knee, CSO seems an obvious seat to add to your roundtable if it isn't there already. That's the title Michael Loparco chose when he created this position at the EMS division of Jabil. I'll stay away from whatever titles you want to use or whether it is a C-suite title at all. I've seen executive vice president of sales, CSO, chief revenue officer, chief growth officer, and many others, and they all do the job just fine. What does matter is that you are involving the function closest to the customer and most vital to the health of your revenue stream in your most strategic leadership discussions.

Remember: The purpose of business is to create a customer. Customers generate revenue. All three of the primary functions I've enumerated—making or delivering something, selling it, and collecting and managing the money you generate—orbit around revenue.

But it doesn't really matter what you call them. It matters that they're included in your strategy. I just want to seat a sales leader who is amply equipped to take a strategic role in selling and who will bring that strategy into the C-suite.

A SEAT FOR THE CUSTOMER

You have probably heard that while an Amazon business meeting may have five people or fifteen, every event includes one extra seat. Visibly, it remains empty, unoccupied. Yet it does accommodate an indispensable presence: the customer. Writing in an *Inc.* newsletter, John Koetsier, of Singular, reports a conversation with an Amazon insider who told him, "One problem is that the customer isn't really there at every meeting. So, what we like to do at every meeting is we reserve a seat for the customer." Of course, the vacant seat is only symbolic and perhaps, as Koetsier himself suggests, even cheesy. Yet he concedes that it visually compels "every meeting participant and every discussion to reference Amazon's customers." Moreover, the symbolic chair embodies an imperative closely associated with Jeff Bezos: "Start with the customer and work backward."[17]

You can go one step further. Instead of an empty seat, you can fill it with a real, live person. Instead of guessing at what the customer might want or need, you can ask them, even if indirectly. You can fill a crucial seat at your roundtable with a person from sales. This person represents the function most directly connected with the customer and (equally as important) prospects who are yet to become customers. Even more valuable is that the sales leadership has the best insights to contribute about prospects in the market who don't choose you. They are closest to the losses, the objections, and the reasons your potential customers selected your competition instead of you. They are least likely to succumb to corporate vanity about how great you are. If you have the right kind of leader in the right seat, that sales leader is the next best thing to actually having your customer in every meeting.

To do this, sales must be fully integrated into your company's leadership, occupying the right seat at the executive roundtable.

CHAPTER 6

The Three Cs of Communicating and Inspiring

In my research and work with clients, I've found that the kind of leader who creates business growth that is energized—not limited—by financial goals not only sees goals and their associated strategies clearly but projects them precisely and vividly for others. An inspiring leader helps others see they contribute to the growth of a business by defining what success looks like and demonstrating for employees, investors, customers, and others how they all benefit from having a place in that picture. They bring vision, strategy, and execution to life by inspiring others and communicating powerfully.

My first book, coauthored with John H. Zenger and Joseph R. Folkman, was *The Inspiring Leader: Unlocking the Secrets of How Extraordinary Leaders Motivate*. We wrote it with an ambitious agenda—we wanted to explain what leaders do and how they bring about high performance in those they lead and manage, and to explain what is required to transform a group that has produced average results into a group producing exceptional results. And while innumerable leadership books promise some version of this, we proposed achieving our purpose by singling out an aspect of leadership that has largely been ignored: inspiration. It was challenging because there may be no fuzzier a topic in the leadership arena. Conversations about how leaders inspire frequently devolve to explorations of personality styles, which can't really be learned, or charisma, which is about as fuzzy as it is inspiring. But our research helped us get beyond that and determine what leadership approaches and behaviors were most correlated with leaders who inspire.

Our sense was that it would be incredibly useful to decode that for leaders. It was also incredibly important because, in the universe of leadership competencies, one quality emerged as more important than any other: *the ability to inspire and motivate high performance.*

This is not my opinion. It is the assessment of 200,000 direct reports, managers, and peers describing 20,000 leaders in an extensive database of multirater or 360-degree feedback surveys. If you want to know how leaders ought to lead, then you should ask those who are led. The receipts were there to prove it. And we audited them in three distinct ways: First, "inspires and motivates to high performance" emerged as the most powerful predictor of whether someone is seen as an extraordinary leader. By a wide margin, this single item stood out from a field of differentiating leadership competencies. Second, when the subordinates of tens of thousands of leaders were asked what leadership competency they most wanted in their leader, their first choice was "inspires and motivates to high performance." Finally, when we analyzed what leadership behaviors were most associated with the highest levels of employee commitment, inspiring and motivating topped the list.[1] So, it was the most desired leadership characteristic, had the greatest impact on employee engagement, and was the clearest marker of a leader being seen as exceptional. I'll take it.

You should be able to conclude from those three points that I evaluate inspiring leadership by the performance and results it produces. After all, inspiring and motivating others is a means to an end. Being a great leader is a laudable goal, and leading well is noble too. But Growth Leaders don't inspire others to high levels of performance just for the hell of it. Nor do they do it because it's the right thing to do. They do so because they understand that inspiration is an important factor in achieving great results. It allows them to galvanize their teams and organizations on strategy and move them to action. An inspiring leader motivates the team to achieve the results necessary to attain the successful execution of their strategic objectives.

Of course, when I work with executives, it's not too useful to say, "Go be inspiring. Motivate people." As I mentioned, as leadership characteristics go, this one, vital as it may be, is among the more nebulous. Additionally, what inspires in different circumstances varies tremendously among people and organizations, which makes breaking it down that much more important.

THE USE OF EMOTION[2]

In that study with my coauthors, we found that those who were most inspiring—the top 10 percent of the group—had the ability to establish a strong emotional connection with their employees. I'm always careful about my use of this term—*emotional connection*—when working with executives. This is not about displaying excessive emotion, oversharing personal information, or getting into therapy sessions with your colleagues. The idea of using emotion as a leader is about connecting with your teams, your managers, and your employees as humans with emotions, not task-focused automatons. It's the emotions that you as a leader evoke within others that enable you to bring out the best in them.

When it was clear in our research that the hallmark of inspiring and motivating others was the ability to use emotion successfully, I was transported back to college. I got my undergraduate degree in communication studies with a focus in rhetoric. I learned about Aristotle's model of communication. It's been about 2,400 years since he outlined the principles of effective communication, and everything since has been derivative. He was clear about how communication and persuasion could move others to action, which starts to sound a lot like inspiring and motivating others. So, we can access some ancient wisdom to further understand and develop the characteristics of inspiring leadership and the power of the emotional connection.

I'm doing my best not to inflict my rhetoric background on you here, and for a Growth Leader to inspire and communicate powerfully, it doesn't require digging deep into Aristotelean philosophy. To make it pragmatic, all we need to do is modernize the language and see how these characteristics show up. Aristotle's three rhetorical appeals are ethos, logos, and pathos.

Ethos is a person's character, how they are guided by their beliefs and ideals. Having a clear ethos builds credibility. Logos is logic. You demonstrate this characteristic through clarity of thought and action. Pathos is all about emotion. It appeals to a person's empathy, and it creates a connection. Together, I call these the three Cs of Inspiring and Communicating.

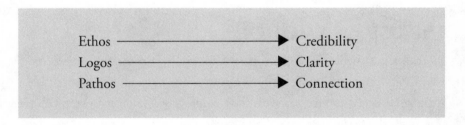

Aristotle recognized that a person's ability to get to the hearts and minds of others was based in large part on how they appeal to others in these three areas. I learned that Aristotle believed that logos should be the most important of the three appeals. That's hardly a surprise for a philosopher and master of logical reasoning. But he taught that all three are important to consider and recognized that humans aren't perfectly logical most of the time. As you'll see, when coupled with the research on emotional connection as the most valuable ability when it comes to inspiring and motivating others, as the maxim suggests, logic makes us think, but emotions make us act.

CREDIBILITY

Ethos is all about your credibility as a leader. Before others will accept what you have to say, they have to perceive you as credible. Some credibility comes with a position or role, such as C-suite or leadership titles. But that title is nowhere near enough. You've certainly seen skepticism of the credibility of leaders who occupied executive roles. As leadership authors Jim Kouzes and Barry Posner say in their seminal work on this topic, *Credibility: How Leaders Gain and Lose It, Why People Demand It*, "Leadership is personal. It's not about the corporation, the community, or the country. It's about you. If people don't believe in the messenger, they won't believe the message. If people don't believe in you, they won't believe in what you say."[3] Credibility is a cornerstone of inspiration and communication. In their research, Kouzes and Posner identified four universal characteristics that, taken together, help us understand the building blocks of developing and improving credibility:

- Honesty: telling the truth and not intentionally misleading people

- Competence: understanding of your business and displaying good judgment

- Vision: having a clear idea of where you want to take the organization

- Inspiration: demonstrating passion and energy

Credibility also comes from your perspective on how you'll grow the business through a combination of all these characteristics. For the Growth Leader, part of what creates credibility is having that vision and compelling, feasible, or innovative ideas for how you are going to lead the growth of your business. These demonstrate your understanding of the market, customers, and the capabilities of the company as reflected in your Five Flag Start. When people understand your knowledge and believe in you to lead them, you are off to a good start.

Conversely, who would want to follow someone who doesn't seem like they know precisely where they are going? As Posner sarcastically states in his TEDx talk at the University of Nevada, "Hi, I don't have any idea where I am going. Want to follow me?"[4] If your perspective is cogent and well received by others, it's a boost to your credibility. If others feel you do not have a strong vision and point of view on how you are going to grow the company, or if you are seen as not having much of a strategy at all, your credibility takes a huge hit.

Credibility, like so many elements of leadership, is not static and evolves over time. As Kouzes and Posner state, "Renewing credibility is a continuous human struggle and the ultimate leadership struggle. Strenuous effort is required to build and strengthen the foundations of working relationships. Constituents do not owe leaders allegiance. Leaders earn it."[5] And leaders earn or, unfortunately, lose their credibility every day.

CLARITY

Logos is about clarity. Logos originally referred to the content of a speech and how it was organized; we might call it *coherence* today. For the purposes of leading growth, the notion of clarity centers on what you say and how you organize what you say. The focus is to ensure people understand you. One of the most common complaints I'd see when reviewing 360-degree feedback surveys was about the leader being unclear and not communicating in a straightforward manner.

Most leaders use too much corporate speak. They lack precision in what they are trying to convey or talk at too high a level for their audience, relying on jargon and platitudes instead of clear meaning. Speaking with clarity requires thoughtful organization and sharing the right level of detail with your audience. People will feel frustrated if your message is too high level and says nothing. And we've all had the experience of getting lost as someone gets too granular and takes us into the weeds. Clarity applies to everything you do—company communications, customer interactions, every email and meeting. Your communication should be clear, your meaning understandable and unmistakable to every member of the organization.

In her book *The Power of Clarity: Unleash the True Potential of Workplace Productivity, Confidence, and Empowerment*, Ann Latham highlights research that suggests that as much as "80 percent of employee time is lost to confusion and counterproductive activities."[6] At first, I thought that number seemed high. I mean, four out of five days a week? Really. But as I considered the amount of time and energy that was ultimately wasted on projects that were never completed or that failed to deliver much value for the business or the amount of rework being done because people didn't have a clear understanding of the expectations the first time or, perhaps most importantly, the volume of activity and time devoted to work that doesn't support the company strategy, doesn't help the business to grow, or is being taken on because someone has a pet project they can't let go of—yeah, that's easily 80 percent. Even if the companies in Ann's research represented the high end of the range of lost time and productivity, the average number was far from acceptable. From juggling and chasing too many priorities to dealing with vague direction and requests to unproductive meetings, a lack of clarity creates significant issues.

Part of the problem is that a lack of clarity often reflects a lack of understanding. Latham suggests that we need more "clarity in the moment," where people confirm their understanding. Without providing that clarity, the misunderstandings only snowball.

While facilitating a strategy session for a client, I routinely heard the term *platform* being used. I heard it used by several different leaders in the meeting. But each time it was referenced a bit differently, with a somewhat different meaning. I was getting lost in the dialogue between the leaders, and I could tell they were too. So, I called a timeout and said, "I've heard you talk about platform in about five different ways, but I don't think any of you are talking about the same thing. Could you each take thirty seconds to write down what you mean when you use the term?" The conversation that ensued was productive; we clarified what platform meant in their business and how each leader was using the term. Taking a moment to draw out clarity made all the difference in their ability to craft a clear strategy to communicate to the rest of the business.

One of the questions I frequently ask of my clients as we are working on anything from formulating a growth strategy to building execution plans is this: "Can you explain that to me like I'm your friend from high school who knows nothing about your business?" That question has opened more clarity for executives than most any other I've asked. It allows them to get away from having to be on stage, from the pressure of having to sound smart or like they know everything. It politely insists that they get away from the corporate speak and jargon and use plain language to simplify their ideas. It helps us break through the fog and see the parts of what they are saying that really make sense and what parts don't. Clarity and simplicity are closely related, and complexity is the enemy of clarity, but this is not about being simplistic. I'm talking about the simplicity and clarity that cuts through ambiguity, provides unequivocal direction, and resolves misunderstandings. Don't overcomplicate your message. Keep it simple. Keep it clear.

As I was working on this book, I would frequently ask myself, "What do I really want to say here?" Sometimes, after a bad writing session, I ask, "What the hell does this really mean?" and "How can I say this more clearly or directly?" or "What is the point I really want to make here?" These are the kinds of questions Growth Leaders must ask themselves as they work to align their teams on strategy, establish expectations and culture, and essentially light the path for everyone in the business.

Communicating with clarity requires discipline to think about what you really want to convey and how you intend to convey it. Powerful clarity is rarely off the cuff, especially when it relates to anything complex or strategic. The best leaders I've worked with spend time thinking about their messages, boiling them down to the essence so they can convey them with the kind of crisp clarity that leaves no question about an expectation, a standard, the work to be done, or the approach to be taken.

Only the gifted few can wing it and expect to be clear and precise in their communication. I've worked with a few executives who were revered by their peers as being among those gifted few. While I'd certainly consider them extraordinarily talented, their talents were exponentially magnified because they were rigorous in their preparation. Too many leaders just say what they are thinking out loud, repeating some of their thoughts multiple times and revising and improvising them as they go. But as it relates to clarity in business, no one really wants to hear you think out loud. They want you to do the work needed to be succinct and direct, and then to get off the stage.

If you think back to flag 1 of the Five Flag Start, a clear definition of success must be inspiring because it must clearly and compellingly define the objective toward which every asset, every behavior, every element of mindset, and every member of the team is to race. Whatever the ultimate vision may be, you and your leadership team need to support it with a crisp, clear picture of success.

None of this is to say you ought to script yourself at all times. Quite the opposite. Clarity does not mean rehearsed, stilted, wooden, or stiff. If you do the work to think about clarity as a primary focus and flesh out your thoughts, you will naturally be clearer.

CONNECTION

Pathos is about emotion—specifically, your emotional connection to others. After all, leadership is a relationship. Because the topic of emotional connection is so easily misunderstood, at the risk of repetition, I'll reemphasize that this is not about excessive emotionality or sitting around talking about feelings. Instead, it's the recognition that, while it may seem obvious, most of your work is with humans. And as I previously wrote for *Forbes* on this topic, "Humans are emotional beings. Few decisions or actions are purely based on facts or logical thinking. If facts alone dictated behavior, advertising agencies would be out of business. No one would smoke, and no one would eat unhealthy foods, or click on Instagram ads. Every decision would be completely rational."[7] Even a few millennia ago, Aristotle—as a pioneer of rational thinking—understood that emotions have incredible power to drive our actions. If you make an emotional connection with those you lead, from individuals to teams to large groups in your entire company, you generate the energy that moves others to action.

It's been more than a decade since our original research for *The Inspiring Leader*. Since then, I've continued to dig deeper into what this looks like in everyday practice and work with executives on how they can harness a wide range of emotions that they and their teams experience to lead growth. Here are five ways to harness the power of emotion to motivate the people you work with to drive better results.

Energy and enthusiasm

Like most of us, you are probably at your best when you feel energized and positive. In this flow state of enthusiasm, obstacles fall to the wayside. You feel the wind at your back. As a leader, how can you generate and maintain this positive state of energy and enthusiasm in others? It is entirely possible. To do so, you must find that energy and enthusiasm in yourself, first. Find your own internal passion for the work and the results you want to see. And then share that passion with your team and your colleagues.

Sharing your passion doesn't mean ignoring the facts, but it does mean finding and sharing the story buried inside the data. This can be tough if you have a serious and focused demeanor, like a chief data officer I worked with. His knowledge of analytics was deep and detailed, but he came across as all facts, all the time. He was not a source of positive energy and enthusiasm for his colleagues. I helped him connect his dry data to the company's big-picture goals and use that story to connect with his team members and their own goals. We found his positive energy by focusing on three questions:

- "What about this (meeting/idea/topic) gives me reason for optimism?"

- "How does it connect to a greater outcome than we are talking about?"

- "How can I share this with positive energy?"[8]

This leader was dedicated and consistent in his efforts to improve. Six months later, he had adopted a strategic mindset. He was able to motivate his direct reports effectively. His peers and the CEO appreciated the broader perspective he had developed and saw him as a better collaborator. Connecting to his own positive energy made him a better leader and colleague.

To be effective, the positive energy needs to be genuine, not forced. Your colleagues and direct reports know when you're conveying genuine emotions and when you're simply acting a part. Acting doesn't get the job done and can be just as damaging as a negative attitude. You've probably heard of toxic positivity and the research by Susan David that demonstrated how negatively it can affect your health. It can negatively affect your team's performance, too.

Your positive energy and enthusiasm should be consistent and maintainable over the long term—the rousing halftime speech or constant cheerleading is not the approach we're looking for here. Vitality and engagement can be expressed in myriad ways, none of which require you to be excessively animated or demonstrative. Convey your enthusiasm by sharing with your team how mundane tasks connect to the big picture. Help them understand how short-term actions can lead to desired outcomes. Positive energy and enthusiasm allow you to be a source of power driving your team to achieve your shared goals and make your vision a reality.

Expressing concerns and anger

Anger can be a valuable tool in business. It can inject energy and focus attention where it is sorely needed. It can communicate a strong sense of urgency. But anger is often misused or overused in business—it can be a front for other emotions such as worry or fear. I've seen too many leaders over-index on anger to their detriment. We may be afraid of failure or anxious about the consequences if plans go awry. When we communicate with anger instead of the true underlying emotion, we become ineffective leaders. But if we dig in and make the effort to uncover what's behind the anger, we can connect with our team in a meaningful and effective way.

Most of us have experienced a boss who uses anger ineffectively. Maybe they yelled or interrupted people or acted aggressively. None of that is likely to elicit the results you are hoping for. In fact, the people on the receiving end of such behavior are likely to feel defensive or fearful and, as a result, they will shut down—which is the opposite of the reaction you're trying to spark. Instead, look inside yourself to understand the true feelings that are coming out as anger. Take a moment, breathe deeply, and ask yourself these questions:

- "Am I angry, or is there something else I'm feeling?"

- "If you answer, 'I'm just angry!' try coming up with a couple of other options. Afraid? Distressed? Worried? About what?"

- "How can I express myself in a composed way so I motivate productive action?"[9]

Anger is often easy for leaders to express. But it's what's driving the anger that is valuable to you and your team as a leader. It takes courage and vulnerability to share these deeper emotions with your colleagues. But you can lead the way and create an environment of shared trust and collaboration. Share your fears and worries. Express disappointment calmly. Listen actively and openly when others share their perspectives. This kind of open communication leads to better team cohesiveness and trust, which leads to more positive energy and a willingness to look at and fix mistakes. With this approach, you will be able to lead your team to achieve your shared goals and move toward your shared vision.

Demonstrate openness

One of the challenges of being a leader is getting the truth from others. This gets more and more difficult as you progress, and it's most difficult for the CEO or chair of a business. It's easy when it comes to the good stuff that people are excited about or pleased with. But most people are incredibly loath to say anything negative about your decisions, to criticize your leadership approach, or to dissent when you are known to have a strong opinion. If people know, for instance, that you believe a new product design is excellent, they will be quite hesitant to let you know they think it's weak. If you express your opinion that marketing is doing a poor job, who will confront you with evidence to the contrary and feel comfortable doing it? How many times have you been in conversations with your boss, be they the CEO or the chair of the board, and not been completely forthright about your opinion because you knew they wouldn't necessarily like to hear it? And how often would they have been more effective—or at least better informed—knowing and understanding your candid perspective?

When you are the boss, and people depend on you for your assessment of them for their professional and financial success, it is difficult for them to share in an unfiltered way. I won't say it never happens. But usually, people are sharing information with an agenda of their own, which often includes not upsetting the boss. I do believe CEOs and most senior executives would be shocked if they knew how many person-hours were invested in orchestrated efforts to avoid upsetting them.

Years ago, I heard this referred to as *fresh paint syndrome*. UK-based author Dave Trott put it this way in a piece titled "The Queen Thinks the World Smells like Fresh Paint": "When people hear the Queen is coming to visit, they want everything to look nice. So they clean and paint it all . . . . Given that everywhere the Queen visits is cleaned and painted, that's all she ever smells. Fresh paint. So the Queen thinks the whole world smells like fresh paint."[10]

Most leaders will say they don't want the proverbial yes-men, people who go along with everything and don't rock the boat. But few back up the claim and behave in ways that encourage hearing about the real perspectives of others. I tell plenty of my clients that they need to work hard to know what people are really thinking. In an article called "Encourage Your Employees to Give You Critical Feedback," I remind leaders that "you will need to go out of your way to invite opinions that others think you may not want to hear." It can be extremely challenging to get people to share their true thoughts about anything that may upset you. "This is doubly hard if you have a history of getting angry or shooting the messenger."[11] Telling them it is safe to talk with you about this may not be enough. You may need to promise them amnesty.

Here is how you can approach establishing amnesty: Let them know you really want their candid opinions. Say, "I want to hear your real perspectives" about the topic at hand. Then, offer safety. You may need to say something like "I promise you amnesty—and that I will not respond defensively or with retribution, even if I don't like what I hear. I value your perspective." Next, make good on your promise. Don't get defensive, and don't hold it against them. After all, you did say you wanted to hear it. Finally, express openness and a willingness to listen to news or opinions that you may not like. This helps you strengthen your connection with those you lead.

Develop talent

The most effective leaders are usually adept at helping their people grow and develop their talents. This is one of the best ways to inspire and motivate people, increase their confidence and engagement in their work, and, ultimately, drive high performance. Leaders who engage and develop their staff like this are remembered by employees as some of the best bosses they've ever had. You and your colleagues can share feelings of pride and accomplishment as they grow and develop their competencies. The long-term investment of time spent coaching and mentoring your people will result in lasting improvements in their performance.

When I ask leaders if they do a lot of coaching and developing talent on their teams, I invariably hear that they do a great deal of it. But the reality is that leaders investing time and energy in the development of their people is rare. This research, from my *Harvard Business Review* article "Sales Teams Need More (and Better) Coaching," illustrates the point: "Leaders reported that they spent a considerable amount of time coaching their direct reports and scored themselves high on their efforts—on average, just shy of the 80th percentile." But their direct reports say "they'd received little to no coaching from their leaders and scored them low—on average around just the 38th percentile."[12]

I have found this pattern to be consistent when I speak with leaders about the coaching they provide and the coaching they receive from their managers. The sense among the employees is that their boss, regardless of whether they are the CEO or a frontline supervisor, does not provide a lot of useful coaching and development. At the same time, most leaders believe they do an outstanding job of it. Asking for forecasts, requesting information, reviewing performance data, telling someone what to do, and pushing for better results aren't really coaching. Leaders, in all parts of a business but acutely in the sales function, spend a great deal of time inspecting performance instead of improving performance through coaching.

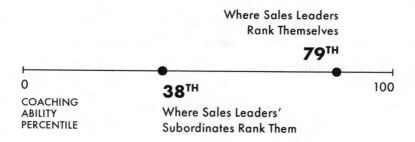

ARE YOU THE COACH YOU THINK YOU ARE?

Where Sales Leaders
Rank Themselves

79TH

0
COACHING
ABILITY
PERCENTILE

38TH
Where Sales Leaders'
Subordinates Rank Them

100

Taking the time to create an emotional connection with your people— investing in them—is an investment in your business. It isn't altruism. People will respond to your commitment to them and your confidence in them with an increase in loyalty and motivation, which will lead to the results you want over the long term. As your employees get better, your results will get better. Everyone wins.

Balance pressure on performance

As the old saying goes, "Nothing brings a team together like winning," and most of us want to be a part of a winning team. Keep goals, objectives, and high performance in front of your team, and sustain the emphasis on achievement as a way of connecting on your shared destiny. Driving a team toward the desired outcomes can create the sense that we are all in this together and can bring out the best in them. Early in my career, my boss introduced the phrase "Results or Bullshit" to our entire team. It was a quotation from a book called *Napkin Notes: On the Art of Living* by Dr. Michael Durst, and it became our motto. We relished both the challenge and achievement of performing at a high level to produce for the organization. I'm sure you have seen that same kind of commitment and engagement rise when there is energy and focus on producing results.

But there has to be a proper balance, and you've certainly seen instances where leaders press too hard and it backfires. In my experience, leaders are prone to misunderstanding the value of pressure and then overuse it, pushing to a point of diminishing returns.

The following figure, originally created by psychologists Robert Yerkes and John Dodson, illustrates how performance on tasks improves with increased physiological or mental arousal. Their research clearly shows that pressure helps us get the job done—but only to a point. Too little pressure and you're in the weak performance zone. This will lead to careless mistakes and a lack of effort, either because it's too easy or because there is too little concern. Great actors sometimes suggest that they always feel some butterflies before going on stage. Their absence means the actor no longer cares enough. But too much pressure will create distress and impaired performance, like an athlete who is too much in their head and struggles to actualize their knowledge, skills, and talents.[13] We know this as choking. Too much stress in any professional situation will mask talent and lead to poor decision-making. Our ability to focus, solve problems, and accurately remember details declines dramatically in the face of excess stress. In the middle, there is an optimal level of stress that produces what we'd call peak performance. The technical term for that zone is *eustress*, which nobody uses, but we all know it as the high-performance zone, which is exactly where leaders should aim to set the pressure to drive optimal results.

Connecting with others by balancing the right levels of pressure allows you as a Growth Leader to set the stage for high performance. This is true for every role and function in the business. But, like so many other areas I've highlighted in this book, it has particularly counterproductive outcomes in your sales organization.

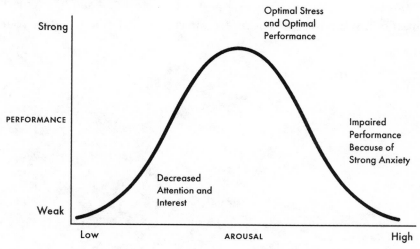

THE YERKES-DODSON LAW
How anxiety affects performance.

During an olive oil tasting in Italy, our guide described this point with perfection as she detailed the process of making extra-virgin olive oil. During cold-pressing, processors had to be attentive to both quality and output. Press the olives too little, and they don't yield enough oil. But press them too much, and the oil is too bitter and may not even be edible. Getting high performance from your people is a lot like making good olive oil. Balancing that pressure is part of how you connect with them and bring out their best.

EMOTIONAL CONTAGION

One last note here on the power of your emotional connection. Research by Fowler and Christakis[14] has shown that a person's mood is affected by the people they associate with. The following figure shows that more positive emotional states clustered together, as did negative states. If you are routinely interacting with others who are in a positive or upbeat emotional state, some of that will rub off on you. The same is true for the transmission of negative emotional states. Moreover, that mood can be affected even by three degrees of separation from people they don't even know. I suspect that the impact is even greater for those who work for you in an organization in terms of frequency and intensity. When a leader is enthusiastic, it can be positively infectious. When frustrated or dour, it can create a dark cloud over everyone.

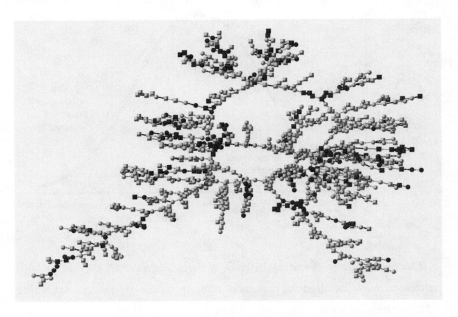

Reproduced from "Dynamic Spread of Happiness in a Large Social Network: Longitudinal Analysis over 20 Years in the Framingham Heart Study," by James H. Fowler and Nicholas A. Christakis, vol. 337, p. 3, copyright © 2008, with permission from BMJ Publishing Group Ltd.

Given this truth, imagine your impact on those who work for you. Whether positive or negative, your emotions and the way you use them to connect with others multiply, ramify, and amplify throughout the business. This isn't a simple matter of spreading good moods or bad. For the Growth Leader, it is a matter of organizational productivity, cultivating high performance, and the level and quality of effort you get from people. It's even a matter of how satisfied people are with their jobs. All of this is directly influenced by how people are connecting emotionally with you and others in the business.

As evidenced by the myriad options you have to express both positive and negative emotions productively, this is not a call to shield or minimize frustration or difficulty or keep things happy all the time. It is instead the recognition of an important need to be attentive to your own emotions and how you use them to connect with others. Do it well and you unlock an advantage that becomes a force in your success.

As you read through this chapter and the approaches to communicating and inspiring, you may have a sense that few of these behaviors, if any, will operate singly or independently. Inspiring leadership behaviors don't exist as isolated variables, and it is rarely the result of only one thing a leader does. Rather, it's a combination of a variety of these behaviors. They all blend to create a signature of how you communicate and inspire that is uniquely yours. There are as many ways to make an emotional connection with others as there are emotions. Ever seen one of those emotion wheels with the complete granular range of emotions organized by major category? You experience many of them in the course of your work, and so do the people you work with. Those emotions inform thoughts, ideas, reactions, and even physical responses. They are always operating in the background. The real key is your willingness to be real with others and put forth effort to connect with them with an intent to bring out their best.

CHAPTER 7

Magnets and Milestones

Following a bad loss where the Tampa Bay Buccaneers looked especially inept, head coach John McKay was asked by a reporter, "What do you think of your team's execution, Coach?" McKay, who was noted for his biting sarcasm, famously replied, "I'm in favor of it." Companies fail due to execution of the strategy. Companies grow when a Growth Leader connects the strategy with how the work is done by their teams or individuals. Depending on which studies you look at, somewhere between 67 and 90 percent of strategies fail to deliver due to execution. While strategy and execution are inextricably linked, they are fundamentally different in how they show up in organizations. It's easy to fall into the trap of believing that as long as the strategy is clear, people will know what to do so that the execution follows.

Larry Bossidy and Ram Charan suggested in their best seller *Execution* that execution is "the missing link between aspiration and results."[1] So, if the fifth flag in our Five Flag Start tells us what we must improve, build, or acquire to execute our strategy, then we are on our way to creating that linkage. Leading that execution of strategies requires leading for results instead of managing tasks. This is a major shift for many leaders.

For all leaders, when connecting strategy to execution, I employ a model called *magnets and milestones*, a simple metaphorical model that offers a bridge from the plans developed in the Five Flag Start over to the execution required to realize the plan. Magnets (these are your organizational and departmental strategic initiatives) define the work that must be done to achieve each goal. Milestones are a means of measuring the progress of that work toward the goal. This simple metaphorical model guides leaders away from falling into the trap of managing tasks and getting stuck in the quicksand of complex project management.

PITFALLS IN LEADING STRATEGY EXECUTION

You can sink quickly if you focus too much on managing tasks rather than leading for results. For many leaders, completing a strategy process can often feel like they have a new toy they want to play with and yet frequently forget to ensure they have the batteries to power it. When I work with executive teams on leading the implementation of their strategies, we frequently discuss the barriers (or lack of batteries) they experience. These are the most common ones I hear about:

Activity focus and urgency for action

Too much urgency can mean getting drawn into the tasks to be done instead of creating the sustained attention on the outcomes that need to be achieved. It's easy to conflate activity and action with making meaningful progress that advances projects and initiatives to completion.

Measures of progress aren't clear

If your indicators of progress are unclear or missing, you will have difficulty tracking movement toward the achievement or completion of a project or objective. Absent these kinds of leading indicators, evaluating performance and making effective course corrections is challenging.

Complicated project management

Planning and documentation should not become an end unto themselves. Your time, attention, and concern—and your team's—should be dedicated less to adherence to a process or model than to producing results. I hear time and time again how overengineered workstreams distract from addressing the real issues in execution.

Perfect is the enemy of good—or even good for now

When working to improve performance or build capabilities, iteration is the name of the game. Low standards notwithstanding, leaders can't get caught up in perfection—or, more likely, allow it to happen on their teams.

Too many priorities

Leaders often bite off more than they can chew to speed up execution. It usually backfires, because too many priorities mean that nothing is a priority. Balancing the desired results with reality is the key. Otherwise, you end up moving dozens of projects forward by inches instead of advancing the most important miles.

Operational issues take up all our time

Leaders can become consumed by the time and effort necessary to run their business day to day. This makes it more difficult to execute on improving, building, or acquiring capabilities needed to achieve the growth strategy. There is a sense that the decks need to be cleared before we can take on these more strategic efforts. But the opposite is true: Those strategic efforts are what keep the ship afloat. Clean decks on a sinking ship do no one any good.

Poorly defined assignments for implementation

If your projects and programs are missing well-defined objectives or goals, your implementation teams may spin their wheels. They may not achieve the outcomes that you expected. Or, more likely, they will complete only part of what was expected, or the project will morph into something that only slightly resembles the original intent.

Thinking you have to do it because others can't

The essence of micromanagement is thinking you are the only person who can perform a task. More often, this attitude is a matter of leaders being unwilling to give up their involvement in something important to them or unwilling to give up the reward or recognition they receive for that involvement.

There is rarely one culprit when it comes to the hindrances leaders face in the execution of strategy. More often, several of these factors collude to thwart or at least slow your efforts. You may have experienced others not indexed here as well. But this list is instructive in creating an approach to focusing and driving your strategy execution efforts.

LEADING RESULTS VERSUS MANAGING TASKS

Leading results versus managing tasks is often a matter of distinguishing what to do from how to do it. When you lead results, you avoid the micromanagement trap and instill a sense of trust throughout the organization that helps people accomplish the tasks they own. Leading for results allows leaders to articulate the strategic initiatives and goals—your magnets—and requires a focus on topics like defining what you need to achieve, what you want people to do, what the performance expectations are, what reflects forward progress, and what priority is more important than another. Managing tasks draws leaders into the particulars of how work will be done, how assignments are completed, how specific issues are being resolved, and so forth.

This is not to say that leaders should never be involved in conversations about anything "how" related. Clearly, some of both is needed. But if you reflect on the issues in the list above, you will notice a shadow of *what* versus *how* throughout. To lead the execution of strategy, the Growth Leader must focus on leading results, which means they create compelling magnets that pull their teams toward the organization's ultimate goals.

When the pursuit of major strategic goals and objectives devolves into the management of hundreds of workstreams, each project nested within those workstreams can easily become an end unto itself. It doesn't matter what management system you are married to—KPIs (key performance indicators), Hoshin plans and Agile development, SGD (strategic goal deployment), OKRs (objectives and key results), or a host of others. If your attention is focused on the framework, then you are already lost in the minutiae. For a Growth Leader, the opportunity lies in your ability to simplify, to stay above the water when outlining the results that you are seeking with the strategy that you have outlined.

Ever since Peter Drucker introduced us to management by objectives in his book *The Practice of Management* in 1954, we've had an unquenchable thirst for models and tools to drive success and help us manage the ever increasing amount of work to be done. Unfortunately, these models have gotten very complicated and, in plenty of cases, overly complex.

In my work with organizations, I have seen all of these models and plenty of others work to varying degrees. And I've seen them fail. A lot. In my view, the failures have more to do with the approach leaders take in using these tools. This became vividly clear to me a few years ago as I was working with a COO and CEO who shared their current approach to strategy execution, which included monthly updates on hundreds of workstreams to support a digital transformation. I was taken aback considering the impossible task of effectively managing hundreds of workstreams and the impact of each one. More than a dozen of their senior leaders said that these workstreams were overengineered and would be unlikely to have the impact they were designed for. Other C-suite executives shared that they were sitting for days in mind-numbing "read-outs and updates" that were essentially valueless. It was a common refrain among managers that the approach was creating busywork left and right that would not make a difference in the results for the business. Too much time and energy were spent using the tools, gathering information, and populating the data, and not enough time and energy were spent focusing on working toward the results. That's what had happened.

Sean Lancaster is the vice president of government and commercial markets for Envolve Pharmacy Solutions. He said this to me about leading results versus managing tasks: "We've all sat through long strategy readout meetings hearing update after update. Most of it is focused on what people have done, meetings they've had, or tasks they're working on. They get way into the weeds, and it's difficult to maintain a strategic perspective. But we had a few areas of focus that were critical to the successful execution of our strategy."

In order for strategy to transcend organizational layers and maintain clarity in the work to be done, the magnets and milestones model is intentionally distilled to the most basic and most critical levels of where strategy meets execution. Magnets help leaders communicate their strategic initiatives, goals, and plans, and milestones mark the progress toward those magnets. This simplified approach ensures that you are clearly articulating where your organization is going and provides the wayfinding signs to track, without getting into the web of tactical management.

Magnets	Milestones
Strategic Initiatives (highest stated goals throughout the strategy)	Indication of progress toward magnets. Nested under appropriate magnet
Projects (complete in support of the strategic initiative)	

The model's ability to deliver clarity for teams was demonstrated in a conversation with Alan Crawford, president of L3Harris Commercial Aviation Systems. Talking to his team during one of our strategy execution sessions, he said, "We are investing $6M in this project. So, when we meet every two weeks, we'll have spent another $250k each time. We need to be discussing the next milestones of progress toward building this [data analytics platform] capability [the magnet]. I want to hear about the challenges we're facing and the decisions we need to make to keep us on track instead of getting reports on all that's been done. We can't wait until summer and realize we've spent nearly $4M, done a lot of stuff, and aren't close to the result." By using magnets and milestones, Alan achieved an elevation (not too detailed and not too visionary) that enabled his team to move and articulated the essence of some of the strategic challenges ahead.

MAGNETS

Magnets provide needed guidance and pull your team toward the stated end goal of the overarching strategy without getting lost in the detail. The first level of magnets is what many of my clients call *strategic initiatives*, a kind of superproject that is designed to address the needs identified in flag 5 of the Five Flag Start. For instance, if your fifth flag identified the need for an expanded product suite to fill a gap in the market, then you probably need a major initiative dedicated to creating that series of offerings. Countless projects will collectively deliver that for you, regardless of the topic—improving the performance of the sales organization, enhancing your customer experience, building a new data center, establishing an R&D team, or acquiring a strategic partner to handle fulfillment. Major efforts that are necessary for your strategy to be executed deserve high-profile attention.

Creating powerful magnets

For strategic initiatives and the projects nested underneath initiatives, as a Growth Leader you must use them to attract your team's efforts and attention. I've seen important projects and initiatives fail because they hadn't been properly magnetized. They were just long to-do lists for teams to complete in addition to their day jobs. There are three necessary steps to magnetize a strategic initiative or project: focusing your scope, finding the right level of attraction, and being selective.

Focused scope

"The power of well-defined strategic initiatives—to help everyone understand and rally around what we needed to improve on—made a huge difference," Sean Lancaster said in an interview. "It focused our efforts on what mattered most and enabled us to look at everything we were doing that wasn't contributing to those outcomes and stop doing them."

You've probably been in one of those meetings where your leadership team created a list of things to get done and then had it transcribed so that you could review it a few days later. I've laughed with clients about reviewing such lists while wondering, "What does this even mean?" about at least a few of the topics.

When you create magnets, put some rigor into defining your initiatives and projects in terms of the outcome you want to achieve, not the activities to be completed. Stress the output rather than the input. That shift in emphasis goes a long way to establishing initiatives or projects with greater focus. It also ensures that these initiatives aren't reduced to checking a box and that they are not complete until the result has been achieved. That propels execution forward and creates a pull to completion.

A company that wants to get more out of its sales team might have the strategic initiative "improve sales performance." To turn that into a magnetized strategic initiative, you might say, "Develop team capacity to consultatively sell integrated solutions at the executive level." This example is magnetized in that it defines the goal with far greater clarity and leaves no doubt as to the outcome you are aiming for: improving sales performance.

Defining success and using the language of outcomes to describe what you want to accomplish will go a long way in determining how your people approach the work. And that's part of what you want your magnets to do. A concise statement of this has been attributed to Charles Kettering, the former head of research at GM: "A problem well stated is a problem half solved." In defining a problem, you clarify the scope of that problem and are drawn to possible solutions. Well defined gets you partially done, because it naturally draws you toward what must be done to achieve the entire goal. Now the team does everything with that kind of specificity in mind. When you put significant effort into defining your expectations and setting goals on the front end of an initiative or project, your teams will have a target they can actually hit. We can adapt Kettering's adage to encapsulate the context of our growth framework of magnets and mile-stones: A magnet well defined is halfway to completion. At least well on its way.

Find the right level of abstraction

Magnets serve as the landmark you are moving toward while also empow-ering your teams to own the journey they are taking. So, there is a risk if magnets become too prescriptive. Your magnets may exist at the organi-zational strategy level as a way to express what you will improve, build, or acquire to execute your strategy. Or they may exist at the level of projects in support of those major strategic initiatives. It is all about understanding the right level of detail for the work you or your management team are defining. To get the right level of detail, you must abstract the problem.

In technology, the term *level of abstraction* describes the amount of complexity with which you view an idea. The higher the level of abstrac-tion, the less detail you'll need. At the highest level of abstraction, you'll view the entire system as a single item, and at the lowest level, you'll see every working part of that whole.[2] Your strategic initiatives at the corporate level form that highest level of abstraction. The next level are the signif-icant projects supporting the execution of those initiatives; these are the two levels to attend to as a Growth Leader. The lowest level, in this case, includes the collective actions and efforts of people in your organization to produce your desired results. You hired them to focus on this level so you don't have to.

Magnets are not a model for cascading departmental goals throughout the organization (even though you could adopt some of the principles). More importantly, this is an approach to leading results and strategy exe-cution at the executive level. At some point, your management teams need to produce the project plans, timelines, budgets, and so forth to complete them. All of this is about how the work will get done. Attending to the right level of abstraction will keep you leading results and away from man-aging tasks.

Be selective

As a Harvard Business School professor, Michael Porter, considered the founder of the modern strategy field, wrote: "The essence of strategy is choosing what not to do. Without tradeoffs, there would be no need for choice and thus, no need for strategy."[3] He was referring mostly to the kind of strategic choices you must make about flags 2 and 3 in the markets you pursue and the competitive advantages that make up your power play. But his guidance is equally valuable when choosing which projects you can take on and when you can do them and carefully evaluating which are essential to do now.

A couple of things rang true for me when working with the company with the overengineered workstreams. It was obvious to me—and pretty much everyone there—that they had taken on too much and that it was showing in turnover, engagement, and stagnating performance. Also, while there would still be plenty of work to be done, there was simply too much for executives to review and lead. They needed a more concentrated approach to help them stay focused on the most important projects or initiatives for the company. Part of the answer was making the hard decision and strategic choice to stop doing many of those things. The other was to come up with a way to be strategically involved with the few projects that would have the greatest impact.

When it comes to magnets, the less is more principle strongly applies. Remember, these are major initiatives to help you improve your overall company performance and build organizational capabilities, not *just* maintaining the day-to-day operations of the business. Work with a number of magnets that you and your leadership team can give sufficient attention to and provide resources to do them well. Then you can move on to another.

Magnets do the heavy lifting

Properly constructed magnets both protect your strategy and can ensure that your strategy is weighted properly so that in the execution phase a clear directional force (your strategic initiatives, projects, and goals) is activated to keep your people aligned. Done well, magnets enable you to provide direction on the primary work that must be completed if your strategy is to succeed. They create focus by defining the work to be done and provide clarity about what success looks like.

MILESTONES

Magnets pull the team forward, always with the singular purpose of achieving your strategy. Milestones mark your progress. They tell you where you are. In monitoring the execution of strategy, milestones tell you and the leaders at every level of your organization where the team is in the completion of a project or an initiative. You and your leaders do not manage milestones any more than a driver manages the markers along the road. Instead, each milestone tells you and your leadership team where the enterprise is and provides a basis for high-level decisions. Milestones are vital to allowing you to lead for results versus manage tasks. They are your most useful tool to keep you out of the weeds and focused on the horizon. This keeps you out of the meetings where you get a readout of progress on hundreds of topics. Milestones create concentrated discussions to advance the priorities you've deemed most important in leading the organization.

Every business has a handful of metrics that determine its success and health, but as Goodhart's law says, "When a measure becomes a target, it ceases to be a good measure." Performance measures should not be an end unto themselves. Too often, metrics become a substitute for strategy. But metrics are not milestones. They don't help to make course corrections, allocate resources, or support decision-making. Milestones do.

Milestones are also not project plans, and they are not about breaking projects down into all the tasks that are required. Instead, they establish the path to results. For any given project, there may be hundreds of discrete tasks, activities, actions, or operations that must be done. As a Growth Leader, you certainly need your teams to be putting together detailed project plans, Gantt charts, implementation schedules, and the like. But you aren't well served by routinely digging into those plans. They represent the wrong level of abstraction for you. On the other end of the spectrum, too many executives will abdicate any involvement in execution, saying they don't want to be involved in the minutiae (and they shouldn't be), but that leaves your organization without the necessary leadership to stay on track and accelerate progress. Milestones are how you stay strategically involved without getting wound up in the details. They help you keep the organization focused on the road ahead rather than on the asphalt below.

Creating milestones

Milestones can be deceptively hard to create because of the inexorable pull to build task lists and establish how to get the job done. Good milestones require some vision to determine the leading indicators—measures of progress that indicate that you are moving toward a successful result. They help you see if you are on track and, if not, how far off track you are. These kinds of milestones are much more valuable; they provide data to make course corrections and keep you focused on leading results.

Good milestones tend to come in the two flavors of empirical evidence: quantitative and qualitative. Both types of milestones are valuable, and you shouldn't dismiss the power of observed changes in the environment or with clients. In science, a mix of quantitative and qualitative data are most valuable in drawing conclusions. When I see leaders struggling to identify good milestones, I'll invoke a question credited to Bob Mager, a psychologist and author of *Analyzing Performance Problems*: "How would you know it if you tripped over it?" Sure, it's a little folksy, but it gets these leaders thinking beyond the tasks and toward those observable or quantifiable elements they would see if their project is advancing in the way they want it to.

Crafting milestones for your most important strategic work is something you shouldn't delegate to your team. Involve them, yes, but it's your vision, strategy, and priorities that are being carried out here, and your engagement ensures the proper direction. It's also a valuable way to demonstrate to your team and the organization your investment in the success of your objectives without micromanaging.

Milestones also require honesty—both up and down the org chart—and a willingness to look at reality. During Alan Mulally's turnaround at Ford, leaders were using the green–yellow–red color coding system during the first few meetings to show how well they were doing. There was an abundance of green. After the first few meetings, clearly sensing that this was not a representation of what was really going on, Mulally said, "You guys, you know we lost a few billion dollars last year. Is there anything that's not going well?" As the CNN story explains, the truth began to come out after that. Mark Fields, boss of Ford Americas, admitted that the Ford Edge wasn't ready to start production because of some technical problems with the rear lift gate. "'The whole place was deathly silent,' says Mulally. Then I clapped, and I said, 'Mark, I really appreciate that clear visibility.'" After that meeting, all three colors appeared on the charts. That new chromatic view allowed Mulally to quickly and accurately see where his team's milestones were being reached.[4]

A CHAIN OF ATTRACTION

If you examine a nonmetaphorical magnet, you'll notice that the stronger the magnet is, the more it attracts magnetic material. For example, if you have an iron plate, you'd be hard pressed to keep a powerful magnet from sticking to it. But magnets also attract each other. You can link them together, and they are forced into a single alignment of poles. But the power of magnetism drops off rapidly as distance increases. If your magnets are too far apart, they don't effectively pull each other any longer. That's where milestones come in. You want your large, magnetic goals to be far enough apart that they are separate objectives, but you need links along the way to keep the forces moving in the right direction. Milestones mark the way, but they also connect the destinations.

Sean Lancaster described this well in a conversation with my team: "I knew there were tons of project plans and project management activity that needed to occur to achieve the milestones," he said. "But as an executive team, we just couldn't dig into it at that level, or we'd spend days each month reviewing it all. We had to provide leadership that kept us all focused on the results. It required a lot of candor, and we had to trust our teams to do the work they needed to. And they had to trust us that they didn't need to justify what they were doing or try to make the results look better than they were to avoid difficult conversations. That kept us all focused on reaching each milestone in our execution plans."

Navigating results

Execution at the executive level is challenging, and you need a way to keep your eye efficiently and effectively on progress being made, on the critical work that needs to be done to bring your strategy to life. Your job is not to execute; your job is to ensure that the magnets are placed at the appropriate distance away from one another and that the milestones are in place to link those magnets. As a Growth Leader, you are setting the magnets that you want the organization to reach, and the milestones will ensure that the way-finding signs guide the work to get there.

Magnets and milestones offer a straightforward, uncomplicated, and effective framework you can apply and adapt. It has the advantage of being simple in structure so leaders don't get caught up in too much detail. You may very well find that for executives managing multibillion-dollar businesses, simply having a framework like this is enough to define and sustain focus on your execution priorities, keeping you properly involved where there are issues with implementation that you need to be aware of and address.

From financial services to healthcare to technology and every industry sector in between, businesses continue to increase in complexity. The way you lead the execution of your strategy shouldn't. If you prefer an approach with greater density, then there are plenty to choose from, although you can still magnetize your objectives or goals, and the principles used in creating milestones widely apply. More importantly, magnets and milestones are not a substitute for strategy. They are an extension of it.

CHAPTER 8

Points of IF

I grew up in Merritt Island, Florida, fifteen miles from the Kennedy Space Center. I watched every space shuttle launch while I was in elementary and junior high school. Our tiny home would shake lightly and the windows would rattle during rocket launches, which occasionally served as the notice to run outside and watch a space shot light up the sky. In the early years of the shuttle, launch days became school holidays. We were expected to watch the launch live. Later, as such events became more routine, we were given just a half day and, later still, only a single period. By the time I was in high school, going out to watch was optional. You could watch on TV in class. January 28, 1986, was so cold—at least by Florida standards—that I decided to stay in. We watched on TV, and many of us didn't realize what had happened until some kid ran in shouting, "The shuttle blew up!" And then we all ran out without pausing to get our jackets.

The space shuttle *Challenger* exploded seventy-three seconds after launch, causing the deaths of its seven crew members, including Christa McAuliffe, the first teacher launched into space. President Ronald Reagan authorized the

Rogers Commission (including Neil A. Armstrong, first man on the moon, and Nobel laureate physicist Richard P. Feynman) to investigate. The commission determined that the explosion was caused by the failure of an O-ring seal in the solid rocket booster due to the unusually cold temperature at Cape Canaveral, Florida—about 31 degrees Fahrenheit at the time of the launch. This failure created a breach of burning gas, which ignited internally, causing the explosion and the disintegration of the shuttle.

For me, that event remains a memory as bitterly cold as the day itself. I grew up a big fan of NASA, and, yes, I understood that riding a rocket into space is dangerous. But as I came to see it, when the Rogers Report was made public, the core of the tragedy was that the fatal explosion was entirely preventable. The problem with the O-rings—that they became inelastic and brittle in temperatures below or even near freezing—was a known issue.

Years later, I discovered an engineering concept called *predictable failure points*. The concept is simple: To predict the odds of failure in any product or system, identify predictable failure points. The process of making such predictions is called predictive failure analysis. The term was once proprietary to an IBM technology used to monitor the likelihood of hard disk drive failure, but today it is commonly used in engineering and other disciplines.

The Rogers Report revealed that the failure of the shuttle O-rings in freezing temperatures was predictable, which means that the O-rings themselves were predictable failure points. In fact, the night before the launch, there was a three-hour teleconference between NASA and engineers for the company that manufactured the solid-fuel shuttle boosters. The participants discussed the effect of the low temperature clearly forecasted for the launch on O-ring performance. Over the protests of some in the teleconference, the decision was made to proceed with the launch.

The predictable failure point was not willfully ignored, and the decision to launch was not an instance of a callous disregard for safety. The Rogers Commission discovered that booster engineers participating in the teleconference presented their data selectively. The only data they used to make their *go* recommendation was from booster flights that had experienced some reported incident. Normal flights—flights that reported zero incidents—were excluded from the data because the engineers assumed that zero-incident flights could not possibly contribute meaningful information about the effect of temperature on the O-rings. They filtered the data, disregarding information they assumed (without basis in proven fact) would be of no value.

In any complex system, including running a business, we need to identify the predictable failure points. We must take them into account when building our strategies. There are predictable failure points in every business. However, unlike the disastrous O-ring failure, most business failure points, when thoughtfully addressed, can be turned into successes.

Because they can lead either to failure or to success, I call these *Points of IF*. The IF stands for *impact or failure*. This phrase recognizes that if the contribution is productive, the impact is positive, and if it is negative, it leads to failure.

The idea is that if you fail to identify Points of IF, your business will suffer. But if you see them, embrace them, and find the path to positive outcomes, Points of IF can lead to enormous success. Every Point of IF you identify requires you to identify and examine it, then find a way to use it.

Although I use the term *points* for simplicity's sake, they often go beyond any single point in time. They may be a series of moments that culminate into a necessary action—taken or not. Executives may have aligned their sales organization with the strategy or not; this is not a single decision or action—and usually isn't a decision or action per se at all. It results from dozens of small daily choices and actions to lead that alignment or look past it. Points of IF are circumstances created by many moments. In order to take advantage of them, you'll have to choose to act both in the big picture and in your daily activities to make sure each Point of IF is creating a positive impact and not a point of failure.

COMMON POINTS OF IF

In my decades of working with organizations, I've seen Points of IF play out for good or ill in myriad ways. But I've noticed that some of them recur frequently, even commonly, in nearly any kind of business. These Points of IF are crucial predictable moments of failure or success. I've narrowed it down to six that seem to appear over and over again. Of course, you may identify more. This isn't every possible gauge on the dashboard, but these are areas where I see leaders often failing to pay enough attention. I've avoided some of the more obvious topics like sustaining cash flow, having a viable product or service, having talented people, and the like. In my view, those are table stakes for leading an organization to that proverbial next level of growth that so many seek. If you address these issues well, some of the other issues, like cash flow or having great products and services, will also improve.

These should sound familiar to you at this point in the book. Too many companies fail to address many of them, much less embrace and harness them. I've written them in the positive—the success version, if you will—because you are now fully aware of the potential success that will likely come if you embrace these Points of IF. Do these things well and you dramatically increase your odds of achieving your growth objectives. Ignore them or do them poorly and you'll pay the price of slow or no growth.

- Prioritize customer value.

- Align your teams with your strategy.

- Connect the executive team to the sales organization.

- Inspire and communicate.

- Focus on growth.

- Use magnets and milestones.

Each Point of IF in this list has been shown to be a crucial tool of the Growth Leader. Without all of these pieces in place, you are leaving money on the table—and maybe handing it to your competitors. With them, you inspire and motivate your team members to work together toward a singular purpose. You create loyal customers who see your company as more than a supplier or provider and instead see you as a valued partner and trusted advisor. You release your company's potential for growth. Consider these Points of IF a framework for knowing where to focus your energy and addressing items in your business that most often predict failure—or enable success.

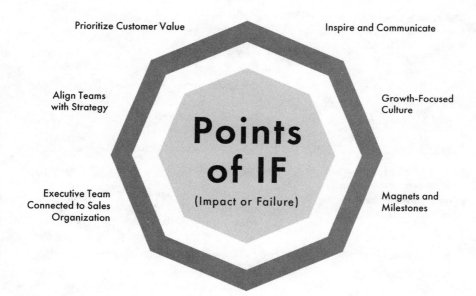

Here is a closer look at each Point of IF and the positive outcomes you can salvage from a potential point of failure. In addition, there is a short self-diagnostic assessment you can use to evaluate your performance.

Prioritize customer value

The sales experience is an important source of value and differentiation for the business, and it is your crucial pipeline for providing customer value. Your products and services must be strongly connected to supporting customer business outcomes, and that connection comes from a sales force that understands, embraces, and enacts the company's strategy. Leaders (including the C-suite) must also be involved in a meaningful way with customers and prospects. Reach out. Speak to them. If you don't know your customer, you don't truly know your business.

PRIORITIZE CUSTOMER VALUE	
1A The sales experience is an important source of value and differentiation for the business. • Strongly agree • Somewhat agree • Neither agree nor disagree • Somewhat disagree • Strongly disagree	Base your answer on . . . • Does the company recognize the sales experience itself as a source of value and differentiation for the business, or is it only focused on the numbers? • Does the sales process give you a competitive edge? • If senior leaders were asked to enumerate your organization's competitive advantages, would they mention the sales experience?
1B Products and services are strongly connected to supporting customer business outcomes. • Strongly agree • Somewhat agree • Neither agree nor disagree • Somewhat disagree • Strongly disagree	Base your answer on . . . • Does the sales team position your offerings as solutions that drive business outcomes for the customer rather than as a series of features and benefits? • Does your marketing reflect how your products and services support customers' business outcomes? • Do salespeople use expertise and insight to help customers think differently about problems, opportunities, and solutions?

1C Leaders (including the C-suite) are involved in a meaningful way with customers and prospects.
 	
• Strongly agree
• Somewhat agree
• Neither agree nor disagree
• Somewhat disagree
• Strongly disagree
	Base your answer on . . .
	
	• Which of the following best describes your CEO?
	  o Hands-off policy (just asks for the numbers and why aren't they higher)
	  o Involved in an ad hoc way
	  o Focused on dealmaking while doing little else to coordinate with sales or support customer relationships
	  o Strategically involved as a Growth Leader, collaborating and supporting the sales organization
	• Do executives, including the CEO, have regular contact with customers, as well as with prospects who chose to buy from your competitors?

Align your teams with your strategy

The company strategy must be expressed similarly by all members of the executive team. Using the Five Flag Start, the company strategy will be well understood throughout the organization, and this understanding will inform decision-making in every function. The company strategy will connect your teams and foster collaboration throughout the business.

ALIGN TEAMS WITH STRATEGY	
2A The company strategy (Five Flag Start) is expressed similarly by all members of the executive team. • Strongly agree • Somewhat agree • Neither agree nor disagree • Somewhat disagree • Strongly disagree	Base your answer on . . . • Would senior leaders describe the strategy similarly? • Are senior leaders aligned, in agreement, and on board with the strategy? • Do executives, including the CEO, talk about the strategy and use it to guide decisions?
2B The company strategy is well understood throughout the organization and informs decision-making. • Strongly agree • Somewhat agree • Neither agree nor disagree • Somewhat disagree • Strongly disagree	Base your answer on . . . • Do employees throughout the organization understand the company strategy? • Are employees clear about their role in supporting the strategy? • Are employees led, managed, and evaluated in ways that support the strategy?
2C The company strategy connects teams and fosters collaboration throughout the business. • Strongly agree • Somewhat agree • Neither agree nor disagree • Somewhat disagree • Strongly disagree	Base your answer on . . . • Does the company strategy lead people across levels and divisions to collaborate on common goals? • Is teamwork between marketing and sales fueled by common objectives and goals? • Does marketing research incorporate feedback and insights from sellers in the field?

Connect the executive team to the sales organization

Your sales leadership must have the right seat at the executive table. Leaders—including the CEO—should communicate the role of sales in executing company strategy. Your sales teams will understand the strategy and know how to implement it effectively. This influences every sales call—and every customer interaction.

EXECUTIVE TEAM CONNECTED TO SALES ORGANIZATION	
3A Sales leadership has the right seat at the executive table. • Strongly agree • Somewhat agree • Neither agree nor disagree • Somewhat disagree • Strongly disagree	Base your answer on . . . • Is the sales leader regularly involved in discussions with the executive team about business growth and direction? • Is the sales organization more distant from the C-suite than other functions? • Is there a feedback loop between sales and the CEO, and between all other functions?
3B Leaders (including the CEO) communicate the role of sales in executing company strategy. • Strongly agree • Somewhat agree • Neither agree nor disagree • Somewhat disagree • Strongly disagree	Base your answer on . . . • Is the sales leader given a mandate to manage the sales function with a focus on customer value? • Do executives, including the CEO, recognize that the company strategy succeeds or fails in every sales call?
3C Sales teams understand the strategy and how it influences each sales call. • Strongly agree • Somewhat agree • Neither agree nor disagree • Somewhat disagree • Strongly disagree	Base your answer on . . . • Does the sales organization target the right prospects rather than pursuing opportunities that aren't a good fit and won't generate significant business? • Does the sales team avoid sacrificing margin and relying on discounting to win business? • Does the sales team identify issues and opportunities addressed by the highest-value offerings, rather than selling what's easiest or most familiar?

Inspire and communicate

You and all your organization's leaders will provide clear direction and guidance. You'll bring out the best in others by developing talent and connecting with individuals and teams. Employee engagement and commitment is high in this sort of connected culture.

INSPIRE AND COMMUNICATE	
4A Leaders provide clear direction and guidance. • Strongly agree • Somewhat agree • Neither agree nor disagree • Somewhat disagree • Strongly disagree	Base your answer on . . . • Do senior leaders, including the CEO, clearly communicate a compelling vision of where the company is going and how the business will grow? • Do senior leaders provide well-defined direction, including what to do and prioritization of things to do? • Do senior leaders communicate openly, thoughtfully, and courteously, inviting questions, discussion, and feedback?
4B Leaders bring out the best in others by developing talent and connecting with individuals and teams. • Strongly agree • Somewhat agree • Neither agree nor disagree • Somewhat disagree • Strongly disagree	Base your answer on . . . • Do senior leaders engage and connect with employees at all levels? • Do senior leaders bring out the best in others by coaching and developing talent? • Are managers rewarded for developing the people on their team?
4C Employee engagement and commitment is high. • Strongly agree • Somewhat agree • Neither agree nor disagree • Somewhat disagree • Strongly disagree	Base your answer on . . . • Do senior leaders inspire people and build enthusiasm to drive the business forward? • Does the company consistently receive high scores in employee surveys?

Focus on growth

Your values must be defined and understood in terms of behaviors that support growth. This cultural focus means your leaders will be excellent role models of behaviors that support growth. With a low instance of sales stigma and stereotypes influencing your decisions, you will connect more directly with the customer, and your sales team will provide strategic value. This must be a company-wide culture shift, not limited to leadership.

GROWTH-FOCUSED CULTURE	
5A Values are defined and understood in terms of behaviors that support growth. • Strongly agree • Somewhat agree • Neither agree nor disagree • Somewhat disagree • Strongly disagree	Base your answer on . . . • Can people throughout the organization articulate the corporate values? • Are behaviors that support these values clearly understood and rewarded?
5B Leaders are excellent role models of behaviors that support growth. • Strongly agree • Somewhat agree • Neither agree nor disagree • Somewhat disagree • Strongly disagree	Base your answer on . . . • Do senior leaders walk the talk and serve as models of what good looks like? • Is behavior that violates company values not tolerated, even from top performers?

5C There is a low instance of sales stigma and stereotypes influencing decisions.
 	
• Strongly agree
• Somewhat agree
• Neither agree nor disagree
• Somewhat disagree
• Strongly disagree
	Base your answer on . . .
	
	• Do senior leaders hold preconceptions such as these?
	
	  o "Sales is all about personality, and success depends on being charismatic, extroverted, and hungry."
	  o "Sales is less sophisticated, skilled, and professional than other departments."
	  o "Salespeople just have to pitch and close to win business."

Magnets and milestones

In order to lead for results, you must have a limited set of well-defined priorities and well-defined measures of progress to drive the execution of the strategy. Your teams will be focused on achieving results and reaching milestones rather than simply completing the tasks in front of them.

MAGNETS AND MILESTONES	
6A There is a limited set of well-defined priorities (magnets) to drive the execution of the strategy. • Strongly agree • Somewhat agree • Neither agree nor disagree • Somewhat disagree • Strongly disagree	Base your answer on . . . • Are magnets (strategic initiatives and goals) straightforward and clear, defining what success looks like for the company? • Are magnets defined in terms of the outcome they are meant to achieve (output) rather than the activities to be completed (input)? • Do you have the right number of magnets (typically three to seven) so the company stays focused on the most important projects or initiatives?
6B There are well-defined measures of progress (milestones) to drive the execution of the strategy. • Strongly agree • Somewhat agree • Neither agree nor disagree • Somewhat disagree • Strongly disagree	Base your answer on . . . • Does every magnet have clear milestones that help senior leaders understand where projects or initiatives stand and make decisions? • Are milestones both quantitative (metrics or measures) and observational (what would you observe to provide evidence of progress)? • Are milestones defined at the right level so senior leaders stay focused on output and results rather than getting mired in operational updates?
6C Teams are focused on achieving results and reaching milestones versus simply completing tasks in front of them. • Strongly agree • Somewhat agree • Neither agree nor disagree • Somewhat disagree • Strongly disagree	Base your answer on . . . • Do magnets and milestones keep your organization on track and allow you to make course corrections and allocate resources? • Are teams rewarded for results rather than metrics; do teams avoid becoming overly focused on progress measures versus desired outcomes? • Do meetings focus on reaching milestones, rather than getting bogged down with task updates and discussions of what's already been done?

After completing all sections, score them using the table below and calculate your totals. Points of IF with lowest scores represent the most opportunity for improvement.

Strongly agree = 4 points
Somewhat agree = 3 points
Neither agree nor disagree = 2 points
Somewhat disagree = 1 point
Strongly disagree = 0 points

POINTS OF IF	A	B	C	SUBTOTAL
Prioritize Customer Value				
Align Teams with Strategy				
Executive Team Connected to Sales Organization				
Inspire and Communicate				
Growth-Focused Culture				
Magnets and Milestones				
TOTAL				

Consider your Points of IF. Go back through this book and pay attention to areas that need improvement and consider how to address them. If you ignore them or fail to see them, your organization may struggle. But if you embrace and address them, they open the doors to growth.

GRACEFUL GROWTH

Michael Malatin, the CEO of Evolution Parking and Guest Services, wanted to grow his new business. This was hardly unusual as a goal, but he put it to me this way when he hired me to consult: "I know we can grow. I know we can get the results. I've done it before, and I got the results. But it was all blood and sweat and tears and snot." I laughed at the face he made as he said this. "It was crazy, messy, and nuts. I don't want it to be like that this time. This time, I want an element of grace to it."

"You want *graceful* growth," I offered.

"Yes. That's it. I know what I want to do, but now the *way* we do it is just as important. Maybe more. Business should not have to be so bloody. Graceful growth is what I want." We talked about grace as the rare combination of speed, power, and coordination. This kind of grace is evident in a business when everyone knows exactly what they are supposed to be doing, have the skills to do it at a high level, and are properly supported by systems, process, and the environment or culture.

Valet parking is one of those many businesses that few of us think about but use all the time. Malatin got into the valet business in the 1990s to support himself in college. The part-time gig led him to build his first parking company, which served hospitals. By 2007, that company was providing valet services to some three hundred hospitals coast to coast.

Valet parking is about greeting people, taking their cars from them, parking them, and then retrieving and returning them. In a busy venue, with cars coming in as cars go out, this process presents a daunting array of logistical problems to solve. And they have to be solved both in planning and in real time.

The business is inherently challenging, but Malatin saw much more to it. When he was parking cars for hospitals, he understood that he and his organization were now in the healthcare business. They—not a receptionist, not a nurse, not a doctor—*they* were the first contact patients and families had with the hospital. Unless you're transported by an ambulance, parking the car is both the first thing you need to do at the hospital and the last thing you want to be thinking about. The valet service has the challenge and the opportunity to make solving this problem the first problem the hospital solves for the patient. Solving it means successfully performing Act I in a drama that is all about a highly strategic, value-adding patient experience. It frames the expectations for what patients and families will experience once they walk through the hospital's front door.

With Evolution Parking and Guest Services, Malatin took his valet parking concepts from hospital to hospitality and created a parking service not for hospitals but for select luxury hotels. This strategic decision meant that his company had to design a valet service that did more than deliver on the logistics of parking and retrieving cars. It also had to create an experience that was seamless with the level of service customers expect (and will pay for) from a luxury hotel. In addition, valet service for this tier of guest must be painstaking in its treatment of what are typically high-end luxury vehicles. This is important to their owners, of course, but it is equally important to the hotel management, who see high potential liability.

Having designed a unique luxury valet parking experience, Malatin needed to create a sales experience to present Evolution to hotel executives, who had the power to buy his concept. He presented Evolution as a partner capable of extending each hotel's standards of luxury beyond its front door by creating an environment of luxury at the literal threshold of the guest's experience.

The most valuable sales experiences help customers with insight, expertise, and approaches and even illuminate possibilities they may not have considered. As a prospective partner, the sales experience was the strategy in action. Malatin and Evolution's sales team worked to help hotel executives think differently about their valet parking providers, to consider the range of issues that arise and how they can be most effectively addressed. Malatin's team sought the opportunities to make that initial customer experience even more valuable. The sales team went far beyond simply discussing the details of how they would provide the service itself. They provided a more thoughtful discussion of the strategic considerations at play when outsourcing the first impression and the initial moments of the customer experience. Those dialogues about hotel objectives served up the company's power play, which Malatin described as "unprecedented talent acquisition." The company identified "the best people, who perform at the highest levels" and gave them world-class training for one purpose and one purpose only: to create "an awestruck guest experience."[1] The immediate, quantifiable benefit for a hotel is a spike in service performance, Net Promoter Scores, and those all-important online customer reviews that competing high-end hotels live and die by. That's where they focused their efforts. The valet service was the vehicle to deliver those results.

Of course, not every hotel is willing to spend on this level of quality in a valet provider. To succeed, they needed to target those customers who would value this power play.

Michael Malatin and I worked together to design his strategy and what he called the graceful growth culture. In many organizations, growth is solely conceived of as relentlessly driving numbers. But Malatin had done relentless before, and now he wanted a far more intentional and strategic growth. He wanted the kind of growth that emanated from a culture capable of producing the luxury level of service that made for a strategic partnership with hotels whose bread and butter was luxury. The capabilities that would allow Evolution to deliver on their promise to hotels had to be built. They were developed with an intense focus on making improvements in nearly every area of operations and creating a culture that established the company belief system. Those beliefs, reflected in the company values—being proactive, appreciation, accountability, and you guessed it, grace—inform a complete set of behaviors for employees from the C-suite to the frontline valets parking cars.

The company represents an evolution in more than name; it is evolving the commodified business of valet parking, but it also reflects Malatin's satisfaction in getting the company to grow gracefully in that all of its systems and processes work so well that the growth provides gratification for the leadership, the team, and even the customer. When a company grows for the sake of growth, Malatin says, it can be a painful process—"very bloody and messy."[2] The quality of life that transactional growth produces for your people is terrible. Create a culture focused on graceful growth, however, and you create a superb staff that loves working for the company. They would all be fitting partners in the work of a luxury hotel.

The graceful growth strategy also allowed the company, Michael explained, "to be able to grow and scale." We are, he says, "systematically growing new hotels and new markets every single month," but it is being done with "grace, like a swan gliding across the water, but underneath the water the legs are moving."[3] The secret is "a lot of planning," the kind of strategic thinking that creates a team, with everybody in on the plan and pulling toward the same objectives.[4] Most important of all, graceful growth was not a one-sided benefit. It was a way of doing business that paid dividends to everyone who partnered with his company.

Evolution Parking and Guest Services now provides luxury valet services to major brands like Waldorf Astoria, Le Méridien, Marriott, Hyatt, and Renaissance and is growing with, I'd say, grace. It's not perfect by any stretch of the imagination; every business has its challenges, and even those I've written about with praise in this book have their struggles. That's inevitable. Only in rare cases does growth seem to come easily. Even then, what we may observe as ease is likely the result of considerable effort and focus over many years of building toward it. But if you are paying attention to the Points of IF that show up for your business and harness them, you will get the strategic, growth-focused results you're looking for.

My intention in writing this book is to help you make your efforts to grow your business easier and more predictable, even graceful—and, as a result, more successful. Many years ago, a writing coach named Sarah MacArthur asked me, "When you look out the window, what do you see that others don't?" She suggested I "write about that, and you'll produce something valuable." Since the early days of my career, I've noticed this disconnect between leadership, sales, and strategy. It's as if each of these important areas of focus operate separately. But for organizations that want to achieve growth, and do it in an organized—not chaotic—kind of way, bringing those three domains together is the way to do it.

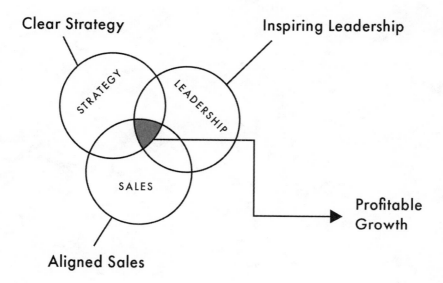

Leading growth lies at the intersection of all three, and more often than not, leaders neglect at least one. When I look out the window after a couple of decades working on organizations, I've seen all those Points of IF in different ways, combining to help leaders build successful businesses or contributing to their failures. That's what I see. If you can see that now too, and you can apply the approaches I've described in this book, you are on your way to being a Growth Leader.

Notes

A NOTE TO CEOS

1. Frederick F. Reichheld, "The One Number You Need to Grow," *Harvard Business Review* (December 2003), https://hbr.org/2003/12/the-one-number-you-need-to-grow.

2. Noel Capon and Christoph Senn, "When CEOs Make Sales Calls: How Top-Management Involvement in B2B Relations Can Drive—or Kill—Deals," *Harvard Business Review* (March–April 2021), https://hbr.org/2021/03/when-ceos-make-sales-calls.

3. Capon and Senn, "When CEOs Make Sales Calls."

INTRODUCTION

1. E. N. Lorenz, "Predictability: Does the Flap of a Butterfly's Wings in Brazil Set Off a Tornado in Texas?," American Association for the Advancement of Science (December 28, 1972), https://mathsciencehistory.com/wp-content/uploads/2020/03/132_kap6_lorenz_artikel_the_butterfly_effect.pdf.

CHAPTER 1

1. Nate Boaz, John Murnane, and Kevin Nuffer, "The Basics of Business-to-Business Sales Success," *McKinsey Quarterly* (May 1, 2010), https://www.mckinsey.com/capabilities/growth-marketing-and-sales/our-insights/the-basics-of-business-to-business-sales-success.

2. Boaz, Murnane, and Nuffer, "Basics of Business-to-Business"; European Business Review, "Sales Growth: Five Proven Strategies from the World's Sales Leaders," *European Business Review* (July 17, 2012), https://www.europeanbusinessreview.com/sales-growth-five-proven-strategies-from-the-worlds-sales-leaders.

3. Scott K. Edinger, "October 8: How to Keep (and Grow with) Your Customers," Edinger's Insights (October 8, 2020), https://www.scottedinger.com/growwithcustomers.

4. Harvard Business Review Analytic Services, "Improving Customer Experience through Sales Revenue Leadership," Salesforce (2021), https://hbr.org/resources/pdfs/comm/salesforce/ImprovingCustomerExperiencethroughSalesRevenueLeadership.pdf.

5. Harvard Business Review Analytic Services, "Improving Customer Experience."

6. Michael Novinson, "It's Official: Avnet Names Bill Amelio as Permanent CEO," *CRN* (September 6, 2016), https://www.crn.com/news/channel-programs/300081974/its-official-avnet-names-bill-amelio-as-permanent-ceo.htm.

7. Novinson, "It's Official."

8. Deyan Georgiev, "Internet of Things Statistics, Facts and Predictions," *Review42* (last updated March 30, 2023), https://review42.com/resources/internet-of-things-stats.

9. Burleigh Hutchins, quoted in Neil Rackham and John R. De Vincentis, *Rethinking the Sales Force: Redefining Selling to Create and Capture Customer Value* (New York: McGraw-Hill, 1999), 23.

10. David J. Collis and Michael G. Rukstad, "Can You Say What Your Strategy Is?," *Harvard Business Review* (April 2008), https://hbr.org/2008/04/can-you-say-what-your-strategy-is.

11. Frank V. Cespedes, "What Senior Executives Should Know about Sales," FrankCespedes.com (October 11, 2016), https://frankcespedes.com/2016/10/what-senior-executives-should-know-about-sales.

12. Collis and Rukstad, "Can You Say What Your Strategy Is?"

13. Frank V. Cespedes, "Putting Sales at the Center of Strategy," *Harvard Business Review* (October 2014), https://hbr.org/2014/10/putting-sales-at-the-center-of-strategy.

CHAPTER 2

1. Capon and Senn, "When CEOs Make Sales Calls."

2. Benson P. Shapiro, Adrian J. Slywotzky, and Stephen X. Doyle, "Strategic Sales Management: A Boardroom Issue," *Harvard Business Review* (November 29, 1994), https://hbsp.harvard.edu/product/595018-PDF-ENG.

3. Harvard Business Review Analytic Services, "Improving Customer Experience."

4. Scott K. Edinger, "Get Over Your Fear of Sales," *Harvard Business Review* (September 17, 2014), https://hbr.org/2014/09/get-over-your-fear-of-sales.

5. Patrick Thomas, "The Pay Is High and Jobs Are Plentiful, but Few Want to Go into Sales," *Wall Street Journal* (July 14, 2021), https://www.wsj.com/articles/the-pay-is-high-and-jobs-are-plentiful-but-few-want-to-go-into-sales-11626255001.

6. Lauren Weber, "Why It's So Hard to Fill Sales Jobs," *Wall Street Journal* (February 6, 2015), https://www.wsj.com/articles/why-its-so-hard-to-fill-sales-jobs-1423002730.

7. Scott K. Edinger, "Sales: Where Strategy Goes to Die," ScottEdinger.com (2022), https://www.scottedinger.com/wherestrategygoestodie.

8. Oriana Bandiera, Stephen Hansen, Andrea Prat, and Raffaella Sadun, "A Survey of How 1,000 CEOs Spend Their Day Reveals What Makes Leaders Successful," *Harvard Business Review* (October 12, 2017), https://hbr.org/2017/10/a-survey-of-how-1000-ceos-spend-their-day-reveals-what-makes-leaders-successful.

9. Capon and Senn, "When CEOs Make Sales Calls."

10. Lisa Earle McLeod, *Selling with Noble Purpose: How to Drive Revenue and Do Work That Makes You Proud* (New York: Wiley, 2012).

11. Daniel H. Pink, *Drive: The Surprising Truth about What Motivates Us* (New York: Riverhead, 2011).

12. Valerie Good, Douglas E. Hughes, and Alexander C. LaBrecque, "Understanding and Motivating Salesperson Resilience," *Marketing Letters* 32 (2021): 33–45, https://doi.org/10.1007/s11002-020-09552-6.

CHAPTER 3

1. Collis and Rukstad, "Can You Say What Your Strategy Is?"

2. John Kiriako, email to Scott K. Edinger (May 5, 2021).

3. Marilyn Much, "Edwards CEO Mike Mussallem Driven by Passion for Helping Others," *Investor's Business Daily* (April 25, 2018), https://www.investors.com/news/ management/leaders-and-success/edwards-ceo-mike-mussallem-driven-by-passion-for-helping-others; Allison Gatlin, "ESG Investing: Why Edwards Lifesciences Stock Is Succeeding by Just Being Itself," *Investor's Business Daily* (November 20, 2019), https://www.investors.com/research/edwards-lifesciences-stock-leads-esg-investing-class.

4. Andris A. Zoltners, PK Sinha, and Sally E. Lorimer, "Why Sales and Marketing Don't Get Along," *Harvard Business Review* (November 4, 2013), https://hbr.org/2013/11/ why-sales-and-marketing-dont-get-along.

5. Scott K. Edinger, "Lead Your Sales Team through Uncertain Times," *Harvard Business Review* (April 14, 2020), https://hbr.org/2020/04/lead-your-sales-team-through-uncertain-times.

CHAPTER 4

1. G.E.P. Box, "Robustness in the Strategy of Scientific Model Building," in *Robustness in Statistics*, edited by Robert L. Launer and Graham N. Wilkinson (New York: Academic Press, 1979), pp. 201–236; quote is a heading on page 202.

2. Wolfgang Mieder, Fred R. Shapiro, and Charles Clay Doyle, *The Dictionary of Modern Proverbs* (New Haven, CT: Yale University Press, 2012).

3. Margie Manning, "GTE Financial Posts Membership Gains after Rebranding," *Tampa Bay Business Journal* (September 21, 2012), https://www.bizjournals.com/ tampabay/blog/2012/09/gte-financial-posts-membership-gains.html.

4. Erik Payne, "Then and Now," CreditUnions.com (April 15, 2015), https:// creditunions.com/features/then-and-now.

5. Peet's Coffee, "Our Coffee Revolution," Peets.com (2023), https://www.peets.com/ pages/timeline.

6. Peet's Coffee, "What to Look for When Buying Coffee In-Store," Peets.com (2023), https://www.peets.com/blogs/peets/what-to-look-for-when-buying-coffee-in-store.

7. Paul Sullivan, "Protecting Andy Warhol from Flood, Fire, and Quake," *New York Times* (September 15, 2017), https://www.nytimes.com/2017/09/15/your-money/ homeowners-insurance-art-yacht.html.

8. Sullivan, "Protecting Andy Warhol."

9. PURE Insurance, "Why PURE," PUREinsurance.com (2022), https://www.pureinsurance.com/why-pure.

10. Roger L. Martin, "The Execution Trap," *Harvard Business Review* (July–August 2010), https://hbr.org/2010/07/the-execution-trap.

CHAPTER 5

1. Jim Collins, *Good to Great: Why Some Companies Make the Leap . . . and Others Don't* (New York: Harper Business, 2001), 41.

2. Weber, "Why It's So Hard to Fill Sales Jobs."

3. The Silicon Review, "Andrew S. Ripps, Bendcare Chairman and CEO: 'We're Committed to Improving the Patient Journey and Making the Healthcare System Healthier for All,'" *The Silicon Review* (2019), https://thesiliconreview.com/magazine/profile/andrew-s--ripps-bendcare-chairman-and-ceo.

4. Scott K. Edinger and Laurie Sain, *The Hidden Leader: Discover and Develop Greatness within Your Company* (New York: AMACOM, 2015).

5. James Clear, *Atomic Habits: Tiny Changes, Remarkable Results* (New York: Penguin, 2018), 274.

6. Clear, *Atomic Habits*, 14.

7. Geoffrey Moore, "We Miss the S-Curves Because We Cannot Stomach the J-Curves," LinkedIn Pulse (May 2, 2016), https://www.linkedin.com/pulse/we-miss-s-curves-because-cannot-stomach-j-curves-geoffrey-moore.

8. Roger L. Martin, "Yes, Short-Termism Really Is a Problem," *Harvard Business Review* (October 9, 2015), https://hbr.org/2015/10/yes-short-termism-really-is-a-problem.

9. Martin, "Yes, Short-Termism."

10. Dennis Carey, Brian Dumaine, Michael Useem, and Rodney Zemmel, "Why CEOs Should Push Back against Short-Termism," *Harvard Business Review* (May 31, 2018), https://hbr.org/2018/05/why-ceos-should-push-back-against-short-termism.

11. Asmus Komm, John McPherson, Magnus Graf Lambsdorff, Stephen P. Kelner Jr., and Verena Renze-Westendorf, *Return on Leadership: Competencies That Generate Growth* (Egon Zehnder International and McKinsey and Company, 2011), https://www.egonzehnder.com/insight/competencies-that-generate-growth-return-on-leadership.

12. Jack Zenger and Joe Folkman, *How Extraordinary Leaders Double Profits: Why Excellent Leadership Deserves Your Attention* (Zenger|Folkman, 2014), https://zengerfolkman.com/wp-content/uploads/2019/04/How-Extraordinary-Leaders-Double-Profits-LRC.pdf.

13. Scott K. Edinger, "The Most Challenging Leadership Job," *Harvard Business Review* (April 26, 2012), https://hbr.org/2012/04/the-most-challenging-leadershi.

14. Peter F. Drucker, *The Practice of Management* (New York: Harper Business, 2012, first published 1954), 29.

15. Bruce Nolop, "The Proliferation of C-Suite Titles Is Insane!," *Wall Street Journal* (March 12, 2014), https://www.wsj.com/articles/BL-258B-2552; Steven McConnell, "C-Suite Job Titles: What Do They Really Mean?," business.com (updated March 1, 2023), https://www.business.com/articles/c-suite-job-titles/; Lorenzo Franceschi-Bicchierai, "Yahoo Names Former Twitter Security Director as New 'Paranoid-in-Chief,'" *Vice* (October 26, 2015), https://www.vice.com/en/article/53dmyz/yahoo-names-former-twitter-security-director-as-new-paranoid-in-chief.

16. Peter Drucker, *People and Performance* (New York: Taylor and Francis, 2011, originally published 1977), 90.

17. John Koetsier, "Why Every Amazon Meeting Has at Least 1 Empty Chair," *Inc.* (April 5, 2018), https://www.inc.com/john-koetsier/why-every-amazon-meeting-has-at-least-one-empty-chair.html.

CHAPTER 6

1. John Zenger, Joseph R. Folkman, and Scott K. Edinger, *The Inspiring Leader: Unlocking the Secrets of How Extraordinary Leaders Motivate* (New York: McGraw Hill, 2009), 5–6.

2. This section is adapted from Scott K. Edinger, "Motivating People Starts with Building Emotional Connections," *Harvard Business Review* (July 21, 2022), https://hbr.org/2022/07/motivating-people-starts-with-building-emotional-connections.

3. Jim Kouzes and Barry Posner, *Credibility: How Leaders Gain and Lose It, Why People Demand It* (New York: Jossey-Bass, 2011, originally published 1993), text on back cover.

4. Barry Posner, "Why Credibility Is the Foundation of Leadership," TEDx, University of Nevada (February 5, 2015), https://www.youtube.com/watch?v=QmMcSBQvQLQ.

5. Kouzes and Posner, *Credibility*, 199.

6. Ann Latham, *The Power of Clarity: Unleash the True Potential of Workplace Productivity, Confidence, and Empowerment* (New York: Bloomsbury Business, 2021), 2.

7. Scott K. Edinger, "An Ancient Formula for Executive Presence That Works Today," *Forbes* (October 15, 2020), https://www.forbes.com/sites/scottedinger/2020/10/15/an-ancient-formula-for-executive-presence-that-works-today.

8. Scott K. Edinger, "Motivating People Starts with Building Emotional Connections," *Harvard Business Review* (July 21, 2022), https://hbr.org/2022/07/motivating-people-starts-with-building-emotional-connections.

9. Edinger, "Motivating People Starts."

10. Dave Trott, "The Queen Thinks the World Smells Like Fresh Paint," *Campaign* (November 24, 2016), https://www.campaignlive.co.uk/article/queen-thinks-world-smells-fresh-paint/1416413.

11. Scott K. Edinger, "Encourage Your Employees to Give You Critical Feedback," *Harvard Business Review* (August 2, 2021), https://hbr.org/2021/08/encourage-your-employees-to-give-you-critical-feedback.

12. Scott K. Edinger, "Sales Teams Need More (and Better) Coaching," *Harvard Business Review* (May 8, 2015), https://hbr.org/2015/05/a-high-percentage-move-to-increase-revenue.

13. W. Timothy Gallwey, Zach Kleinman, and Pete Carroll, *The Inner Game of Tennis: The Classic Guide to the Mental Side of Peak Performance* (New York: Random House, 1997).

14. Pam Belluck, "Strangers May Cheer You Up, Study Says," *New York Times* (December 4, 2008), https://www.nytimes.com/2008/12/05/health/05happy-web.html.

CHAPTER 7

1. Larry Bossidy, Ram Charan, and Charles Burck, *Execution* (New York: Random House, 2009), 19.

2. PCMag Encyclopedia, "Level of Abstraction," PCMag (2023), https://www.pcmag.com/encyclopedia/term/level-of-abstraction.

3. Michael E. Porter, "What Is Strategy?," *Harvard Business Review Magazine* (November–December 1996), https://hbr.org/1996/11/what-is-strategy?

4. Alex Taylor III, "Fixing up Ford," CNN Money (May 12, 2009), https://money.cnn.com/2009/05/11/news/companies/mulally_ford.fortune/.

CHAPTER 8

1. Eric Grundhoefer, "Valet Parking and Front Door Services with Evolution PGS' Michael Malatin," *Becoming Legends* podcast (September 1, 2021), found on Spotify, https://open.spotify.com/episode/05LYngSAOMeKC26EycwrWU.

2. Grundhoefer, "Valet Parking and Front Door Services."

3. Grundhoefer, "Valet Parking and Front Door Services."

4. Grundhoefer, "Valet Parking and Front Door Services."

Index

Acknowledgments

The ideas and content for this book developed like an old-fashioned photograph in solution. Slowly and in patches. It took five years, including three complete rewrites, and my early notes on these topics go back a decade. I'm grateful for those who helped me along the way. Like the credits in a movie, this is where I get to recognize the people who played an important role in bringing this book to life.

Mentors and colleagues Blair Enns and Whitney Johnson helped me to hone my vision and identify the unique blend of strategy, leadership, and sales that forms the foundation for this book. Their counsel allowed me to see how the intersection of these three fields and my background and knowledge could best be applied to help others. John Davis, Barbara Williamson, Mary Coburn, Ken Maddox, Chris Abramson, John Rovens, Neil Rackham, Jack Zenger, and Joe Folkman shaped my understanding of what separates excellence from average in the areas of strategy, leadership, and sales. I'm grateful for the opportunities and the lessons.

In the early stages of research and writing, Amy Gallo helped me outline my hypothesis and focus my ideas. Amy Humble and Sue Barlow managed the research to fortify the concepts and provide strong support for the book. Amy Humble's ongoing counsel in elevating and building on the ideas for this book proved valuable at every turn. Alan Axelrod helped me to tell the stories, and Amy Jameson clarified and refined ideas so that they were ready for prime time.

Any business book is intensely boring without real-life examples. A special thanks to Bill Amelio, Ross Buchmueller, Alan Crawford, Bob Dutkowsky, Robin Glover-Faure, John Kiriako, Sean Lancaster, Eric Lauterbach, Michael Loparco, Mike Mussallem, Michael Malatin, Jake Orville, and Andrew Ripps. I'm grateful for your willingness to allow me to use your stories, quotations, and successes to illustrate the main ideas in *The Growth Leader*.

I may still be working on this book if it weren't for my editor Nathan True, who, at my request, eviscerated the manuscript when it still wasn't hitting the bullseye. It was then he said, "You know what you want to say and how you want to say it." And he encouraged me to rewrite the book with that in mind. He was right. About ninety days later, the book was done.

Thanks to my agent, John Willig, for helping me find a spectacular publisher in Fast Company Press and Greenleaf Book Group. If Carrie Jones and Daniel Sandoval at GBG hadn't been extraordinarily patient with the creative process, this book wouldn't have made it to you. Brian Welch managed this project and production with great precision, and Morgan Robinson was terrific in fine-tuning all the content as lead editor. Chase Quarterman nailed the cover design.

It's amazing to me how much work goes into making a book successful after it's written. I am particularly grateful to the exceptional team at Book Highlight for helping me get this book into the hands of Growth Leaders everywhere.

I'll close these acknowledgments by thanking the most important people in my life: my wife, Christy, and our children, Ava and Vivienne. You are a wish come true. Thank you for being a constant reminder to me of what matters most.

About the Author

Clients in the Fortune 50 and across the globe trust Scott K. Edinger as their premier consultant for leading business growth. Scott has worked with CEOs and senior leaders to develop pragmatic strategies and execute approaches to drive top- and bottom-line results. He has written three books and over a hundred articles in *Forbes* and *Harvard Business Review*, among other prominent publications.

As a consultant, author, advisor, and speaker, Scott creates positive change for clients and is recognized as an expert in the intersection of leadership, strategy, and sales.

He is the best-selling author of *The Growth Leader: Strategies to Drive the Top and Bottom Lines* (Fast Company Press, 2023), as well as co-author of *The Hidden Leader: Discover and Develop Greatness Within Your Company* (AMACOM, 2015) and *The Inspiring Leader: Unlocking the Secrets of How Extraordinary Leaders Motivate* (McGraw Hill, 2009). His *Harvard Business Review* article "Making Yourself Indispensable" has been called a "classic in the making." Scott's work has been published in the *HBR Guide to Your Professional Growth* and the *HBR Guide to Being More Productive*.

Scott has served as an affiliate faculty member for the University of North Carolina Kenan-Flagler Business School. He received a BS in communication studies and rhetoric from Florida State University, where he sat on alumni committees including the Board of the College of Communication and Information, as well as the Seminole Torchbearers.

An extensive traveler and avid football fan, Scott prioritizes experiences above all. He has bungee-jumped into a New Zealand canyon, supported his Seminoles at six national championship games, and performed with the Mormon Tabernacle Choir (despite not sharing their religious affiliation or ability to read music). He and his family live in Tampa, Florida.

Become a Growth Leader.

Connect strategy, leadership, and sales.

Find valuable resources for achieving growth:

- Published articles
- Video courses
- Newsletter archive
- Case studies
- Actionable advice

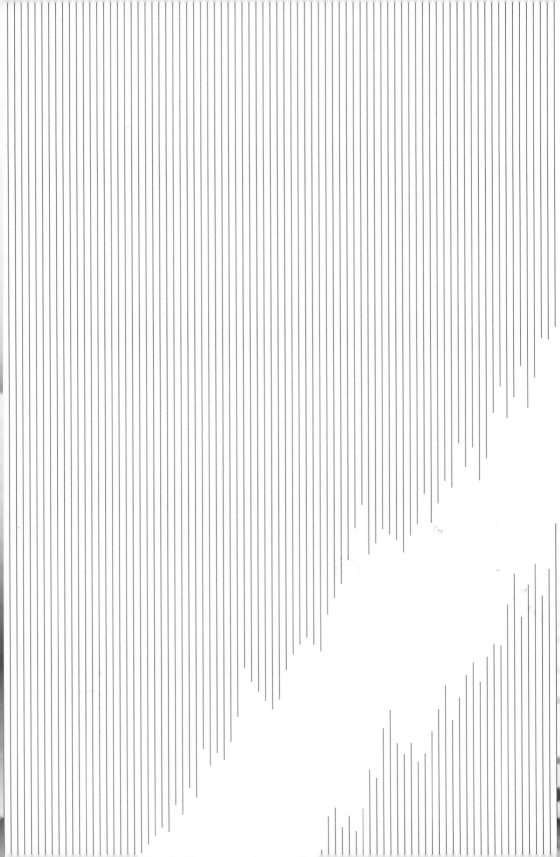